Building React Apps with Server-Side Rendering

Use React, Redux, and Next to Build Full Server-Side Rendering Applications

Mohit Thakkar

D1293064

Apress®

Building React Apps with Server-Side Rendering

Mohit Thakkar
Vadodara, Gujarat, India

ISBN-13 (pbk): 978-1-4842-5868-2   ISBN-13 (electronic): 978-1-4842-5869-9
https://doi.org/10.1007/978-1-4842-5869-9

Managing Director, Apress Media LLC: Welmoed Spahr
Acquisitions Editor: Louise Corrigan
Development Editor: James Markham
Coordinating Editor: Nancy Chen

Cover designed by eStudioCalamar

Cover image designed by Freepik (www.freepik.com)

Distributed to the book trade worldwide by Springer Science+Business Media New York, 1 New York Plaza, New York, NY 10004. Phone 1-800-SPRINGER, fax (201) 348-4505, e-mail orders-ny@springer-sbm.com, or visit www.springeronline.com. Apress Media, LLC is a California LLC and the sole member (owner) is Springer Science + Business Media Finance Inc (SSBM Finance Inc). SSBM Finance Inc is a **Delaware** corporation.

For information on translations, please e-mail rights@apress.com, or visit http://www.apress.com/rights-permissions.

Apress titles may be purchased in bulk for academic, corporate, or promotional use. eBook versions and licenses are also available for most titles. For more information, reference our Print and eBook Bulk Sales web page at http://www.apress.com/bulk-sales.

Any source code or other supplementary material referenced by the author in this book is available to readers on GitHub via the book's product page, located at www.apress.com/9781484258682. For more detailed information, please visit http://www.apress.com/source-code.

Printed on acid-free paper

Dedicated to Richard Matthew Stallman, the man who started the free software movement in order to give software users the freedom to use the software, to study and modify the software, and to redistribute copies of it with or without modification. His work on the GNU project is highly appreciated by the open source community.

Table of Contents

About the Author

Mohit Thakkar is a software engineer with a multinational company. He has a bachelor's degree in computer engineering and is the author of several independently published titles, including *Artificial Intelligence, Beginning Machine Learning in iOS, Data Mining & Business Intelligence, iOS Programming*, and *Mobile Computing & Wireless Communication*. He has also published a research paper titled "Remote Health Monitoring using Implantable Probes to Prevent Untimely Death of Animals" in the *International Journal of Advanced Research in Management, Architecture, Technology and Engineering*.

About the Technical Reviewer

Alexander Chinedu Nnakwue has a background in
mechanical engineering from the University of Ibadan,
Nigeria, and has been a front-end developer for over three
years working on both web and mobile technologies. He also
has experience as a technical author, writer, and reviewer.
He enjoys programming for the Web, and occasionally, you
can also find him playing soccer. He was born in Benin City
and is currently based in Lagos, Nigeria.

Acknowledgments

The completion of this book could not have been possible without the contribution of numerous people whose names may not all be cited. Their contributions are sincerely appreciated and acknowledged. However, I would like to take this opportunity to express my gratitude particularly to the following:

Louise Corrigan, Senior Editor at Apress, and **James Markham**, Development Editor at Apress, who saw potential in the idea behind the book. They helped kick-start the book with their intuitive suggestions and made sure that the content quality of the book remains uncompromised.

Alexander Nnakwue, Technical Reviewer of the book, who made sure that the practical aspects of the book are up to the mark. His insightful comments have been of great help in the refinement of the book.

Nancy Chen, Coordinating Editor at Apress, who made sure that the process from penning to publishing the book remains smooth and hassle-free.

Family, friends, and mentors, who have always been supportive of my aspirations and have guided me throughout my journey.

You, who wish to refine your skills by reading this book so that you can make a difference in the lives of those around you. You encourage me to contribute toward collaborative education.

Thank you!

Introduction

With the popularity of frameworks such as Node, React, and Angular, web developers tend to render everything on the client-side, but there are several disadvantages to this approach. To protect sensitive information and optimize response times, developers might want to add server-side rendering to their applications. This book demonstrates how a React application can be rendered on the server-side using frameworks such as Next and Redux.

The book starts with the basic introduction to JavaScript, followed by the introduction to React. Once the reader is aware of both these concepts, the Next framework is introduced. The reader will then learn how to integrate Next to a React application in order to render content on the server-side. The reader will also learn about state management using Redux, unit testing using Jest, and deployment using Docker. At the end of this book, the reader will have all the knowledge necessary to build and deploy a fully server-side rendered application with scripts for unit testing.

To learn more, start reading right away.

CHAPTER 1

JavaScript Prerequisites

This chapter provides insight on JavaScript fundamentals that are necessary in order to start working with React. The purpose of this chapter is to introduce you to the basic programming paradigm followed in JavaScript so that you can better understand React when it is introduced in the following chapter.

Even if you are new to JavaScript, you need not worry as this chapter shall provide you with all the knowledge you need to get started. You will begin with learning simpler concepts such as constants, variables, and control loops and will go all the way learning sophisticated topics such as rest parameters, spread syntax, HTTP requests, and promises. By the end of this chapter, you will have a thorough understanding of the language and will be able to start building web applications with JavaScript.

Introduction to JavaScript

JavaScript is one of the most popular languages for web development, and it is essential to learn this language in order to create applications that run on web browsers. Apart from web applications, JavaScript can also be used to create desktop, mobile, as well as server-side applications using various frameworks like Meteor, React Native, and Node.js. However, we will focus on web applications for the scope of this chapter.

JavaScript was created by Brendan Eich in the year 1995 and was standardized by ECMA (European Computer Manufacturers Association) in 1997. As a result, JavaScript is also known as ECMAScript (ES). As the web browsers developed over time, so did JavaScript with the release of ES3 in 1999, ES5 in 2009, and ES6 in 2015. After ES6, there have been minor updates to JavaScript every year, but ES6 is by far the latest major release.

Let us now set up our development environment so that we can begin with practical examples on JavaScript programming.

1

© Mohit Thakkar 2020
M. Thakkar, *Building React Apps with Server-Side Rendering*, https://doi.org/10.1007/978-1-4842-5869-9_1

Setting Up the Environment

In order to start programming with JavaScript, I'll be using the Visual Studio Code editor which can be downloaded from https://code.visualstudio.com/download. However, you can use any editor of your choice.

Once the editor is up and running, we will create our starter workspace with index. html file. This file will contain our page template and a reference to our JavaScript file (index.js) which will reside in scripts folder. We will use <script> tag to link our JavaScript file with our HTML template. If you want to add styling to your page template, you can also add a css file (style.css) under the css folder and add a reference to it in index.html file using <Link> tag. Your folder structure should look similar to that shown in Figure 1-1.

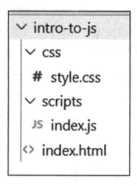

Figure 1-1. *Folder Structure for Starter Workspace*

Talking about individual files, index.html should contain the following code:

```
<html>
 <head>
  <title>intro-to-js</title>
  <link rel="stylesheet" type="text/css"
        href="css/style.css"></script>
 </head>
 <body>
  <h1>Introduction to JavaScript</h1>
  <hr/>
```

```
<div id="ResultContainer"></div>
<script type="text/javascript"
        src="scripts/index.js"></script>
</body>
</html>
```

Here, we have added reference to our JavaScript file (index.js) and css file (style. css). Other than that, the template contains a page header and a section that we will manipulate using JavaScript code. Let us now check if the reference to JavaScript file is working. To do so, add the following code to index.js file:

```
var ResultContainer = document.getElementById("ResultContainer");

ResultContainer.innerHTML = "Setting up the environment!";
```

Note that we have used JavaScript's getElementById() method to fetch a section from the template and then altered its text by setting the innerHTML property. You can also use getElementsByClassName() method and getElementsByTagName() method in order to access elements by class name and tag name. Since we already set the ID property of the <div> element in our HTML template, we used getElementById() method to fetch the section. We initially stored a reference to this section in a variable and then accessed its property using the variable. This is particularly useful when we have multiple properties to alter. You might not want to go and search for the section every time you want to modify a property. Hence, it is always a good programming practice to store references in variables if you are going to need it multiple times.

You can add the following code to the css file (style.css) in order to apply styling to the HTML template:

```
body{
    margin-top:20px;
    margin-left:20px;
}

h1{
    font-size:50px;
}

#ResultContainer{
    margin-top:30px;
    padding:10px;
```

```
    width:450px;
    height:200px;
    border:1px solid black;
    font-size:30px;
}
```

Now let us run our project and see the output. Visual Studio Code does not have a built-in method to run HTML files in browser. Hence, we will have to do some configurations to run our project. Check the documentation for the editor that you are using to find help on launch configurations. If you are using Visual Studio Code, the following steps should help you get started:

1. Press Ctrl+Shift+P to open the Command Palette.

2. Type "config" and select the "Tasks: Configure Task" command to open tasks.json.

3. If tasks.json file does not exist, the editor will ask you to create one with default template. Go ahead with "others" template.

4. Replace the tasks.json file content with following code:

```
{
  "version": "2.0.0",
  "command": "Chrome",
  "windows": {
            "command": "C:\\Program Files (x86)\\Google\\Chrome\\
            Application\\chrome.exe"
            },
  "args": ["${file}"],
  "group": {
            "kind": "build",
            "isDefault": true
        }
    }
```

The preceding process is shown graphically in Figure 1-2. Note that the figure shows the code that is generated by default. We will need to change it to the abovementioned code to configure the launch setting for our application.

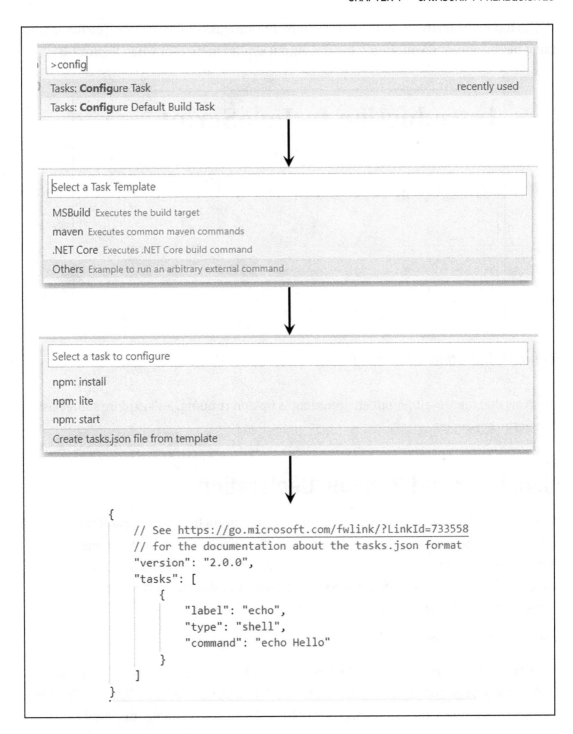

Figure 1-2. *Launch Configuration*

To test the configuration, open index.html file and press Ctrl+Shift+B. The file should open in Chrome, and you should see the output similar to that shown in Figure 1-3.

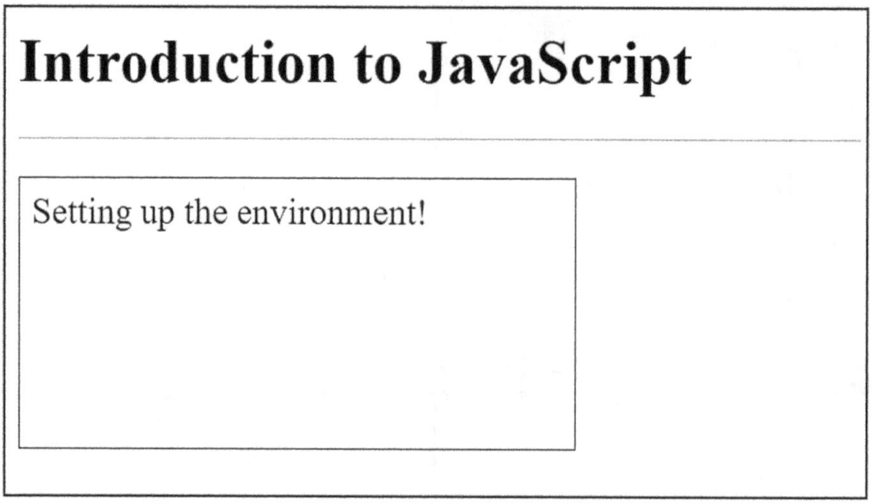

Introduction to JavaScript

Setting up the environment!

Figure 1-3. *Output for Starter Project*

Now that our development environment is up and running, let's explore some basic JavaScript concepts.

Constants and Variable Declaration

Constants are identifiers whose value remains same throughout the scope of the program. On the other hand, variables are identifiers whose value can be changed at any time. One thing to note is that you can declare a variable and initialize it later in the code, but in case of constants, you have to assign a value during the declaration itself. A constant can be declared by using "const" keyword. For example:

```
const weightInKilos = 100;
```

Variables in JavaScript can be declared using either "let" or "var" keyword. While both of these keywords are used for variable declaration, there is a significant difference in scope of variables declared using each of these keywords. Variables declared with "var" keyword are accessible throughout the program, whereas variables declared using "let" keyword are only available in the block in which they are declared. Let us understand this with an example:

```
...
if(true){
 let letVariable = "Variable using let";
}
ResultContainer.innerHTML =  letVariable;
```

If you try to execute the preceding piece of code, you might get an error in the console stating that "letVariable is not defined". This is because you are trying to access letVariable outside its scope. Change the code to the following and you should see the output similar to Figure 1-4:

```
...
if(true){
 var varVariable = "Variable using var";
}
ResultContainer.innerHTML =  varVariable;
```

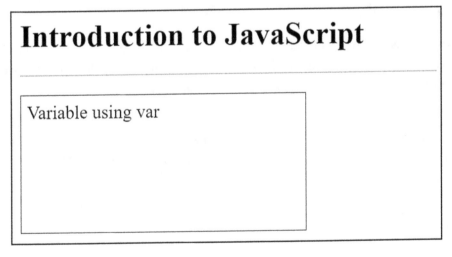

Figure 1-4. *Variable Declaration Using let and var*

Another difference between let and var is that if you try to access a "let" variable before its declaration, the system will throw an undefined error, but in case of a "var" variable, the system will not throw any error. For example, consider the piece of code in Figure 1-5. The last two lines might give you error for accessing a variable that's never declared. However, the first two lines will give you no errors. We would always want the system to throw us an error when we are trying to access a variable before its declaration. Thus, it is always a good practice to use the "let" keyword instead of "var" keyword to declare variables.

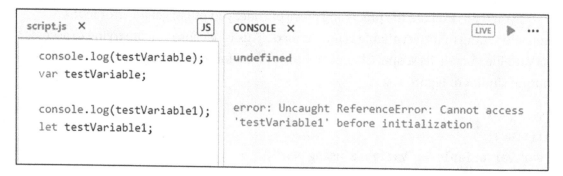

Figure 1-5. *let vs. var*

Rest Parameter

Rest parameter is a feature of JavaScript that was introduced in ES6. It lets us handle multiple function input parameters as an array. It is particularly helpful in scenarios where the number of input parameters to a function is indefinite.

Note   ES6 is the sixth version of ECMAScript and was created to standardize JavaScript. Since it was published in 2015, it is also known as ECMAScript 2015.

Let us understand this with the help of the following example:

```
...
function sum(...inputs) {
 var result = 0;
 for(let i of inputs){
  result += i;
 }
 return result;
}
ResultContainer.innerHTML = sum(5, 10, 5, 5);
```

This should give you an output of "25" on your HTML template. Now let us understand what is happening here. When we declare a function with rest parameter and invoke it, JavaScript automatically takes in all the arguments we pass to the function and clubs it into an array. The function can then iterate through the array and perform operations on all the input elements supplied. Rest parameter can also be used with regular parameters. However, rest parameter should always be the last argument so that JavaScript can collect all the remaining elements and club it into an array. Consider the following example:

```
...
function sum(input1, input2, ...remainingInputs) {
 var result = input1 + input2;
 for(let i of remainingInputs){
  result += i;
 }
 return result;
}
ResultContainer.innerHTML = sum(5, 10, 5, 5);
```

The preceding piece of code will also give you an output of "25" on your HTML template. The only difference here is that only the last two input parameters will be considered as rest parameters, whereas the first two are regular parameters. One of the major benefits of rest parameter is that array operations such as filter, sort, pop, push, reverse, and so on can easily be performed on input parameters.

Destructuring and Spread Syntax

Destructuring is another feature of JavaScript that was introduced in ES6 and is exactly opposite of rest parameter. While rest parameter is about assigning multiple values to a single array, destructuring is about fetching values from a single array or an object and assigning it to multiple variables. Let us understand this with the help of an example:

```
...
let fruits = ['Apple', 'Watermelon', 'Grapes'];
let [fruit1, fruit2, fruit3] = fruits;

ResultContainer.innerHTML = fruit2;
```

The preceding piece of code will give you "Watermelon" as output. This is because when we use destructuring syntax (variables in square brackets separated by commas on left and an array or object on right), JavaScript automatically extracts values from the array on the right-hand side and starts assigning them to the variables on the left-hand side. Note that the values are assigned from left to right. So, for instance, if there are two variables on the left-hand side and four array elements on the right-hand side, then the first two values from the array will be assigned to the variables and the last two values will be left out. On the contrary, if there are four variables on the left-hand side and just two array elements on the right-hand side, the values will be assigned to the first two variables and the last two variables will be undefined.

We can also skip some array elements while assigning it to variables. To do so, add an extra comma separator on the left-hand side. Consider the following example:

```
...
let fruits = ['Apple', 'Watermelon', 'Grapes'];
let [fruit1, , fruit2] = fruits;

ResultContainer.innerHTML = fruit2;
```

This time, the output that will be displayed on your HTML template will be "Grapes". This is because when JavaScript tries to find the second variable for assigning second array element, it finds a null entry because of the comma separator and skips that particular array element. Another interesting thing you can do with destructuring is that you can assign first few array elements to separate variables and assign remaining array elements to a single variable using the rest parameter syntax. Have a look at the following example to get a better understanding:

```
...
let fruits = ['Apple', 'Watermelon', 'Grapes',
              'Guava'];
let [fruit1, ...OtherFruits] = fruits;
ResultContainer.innerHTML = OtherFruits;
```

The preceding piece of code will give you "Watermelon, Grapes, Guava" as output because the rest parameter syntax will assign all the remaining array elements to the "OtherFruits" variable.

Objects can be destructured in a similar way to arrays with the only exception being the use of curly brackets instead of square brackets on the left-hand side to specify variables. Consider the following example of destructuring object:

```
...
let Fruits = {Fruit1: 'Apple', Fruit2: 'Watermelon'};
let {Fruit1, Fruit2} = Fruits;

ResultContainer.innerHTML = Fruit1;
```

The preceding piece of code will give you "Apple" as output. Let us now try to use destructuring in functions. We will try to pass an array as input parameter and destructure it in the function definition. Please look at the following piece of code:

```
...
function sum(a, b, c){
    return a+b+c;
}

let input = [5,9,6];
ResultContainer.innerHTML = sum(...input);
```

The output of the preceding code should be "20". What we are doing here is exactly opposite of rest parameter. We are creating a single array of input elements and passing it directly into a function that takes in three different parameters. The function declaration will be similar to that of a regular function. However, notice the syntax that we are using while calling the function (the three dots before the parameter name). This is known as spread syntax and this will do all the work for us. It is identical to the syntax of rest parameter. However, if you use it while calling the function, it will work in an opposite manner. So, instead of collecting input parameters and clubbing it into an array, it will destructure the array of input parameters and assign the values to the variables mentioned in the function declaration. You can also use the rest parameter and spread syntax at the same time. The manner in which it will behave will depend on the context. Let us now look at control loops.

Control Loops

JavaScript provides multiple ways to iterate through loops. Let us look at each one of them with examples.

for

The for loop takes in three parameters: the first parameter is for the initialization of the control variable, the second one is the condition that provides entry to the loop if true, and the last one is increment or decrement parameter that will modify the value of control variable in each loop. These three parameters are followed by the body of the loop:

```
...
for(let i=0;i<8;i++){
    if(i==1){
        continue;
    }
    console.log("i: " + i);
    if(i==4){
        break;
    }
}
```

We can use break and continue operators with all kinds of JavaScript loops. The continue operator is used to skip the remaining statements from the body of the loop and skip to the next iteration, whereas the break operator is used to terminate all the remaining iterations of the loop.

Notice the preceding piece of code and its output in Figure 1-6. The loop is conditioned to run for eight iterations and print the number of iteration in each execution. However, for the second iteration, the if condition before the print statement in the body of the loop will evaluate to true and the execution of continue operator will make the loop jump to the next iteration. Hence, we do not see the value "1" in the output. Similarly, for the fifth iteration, the if condition after the print statement will evaluate to true and the execution of break operator will terminate the remaining iterations of the loop. Thus, we do not see remaining values after "4" printed in the output.

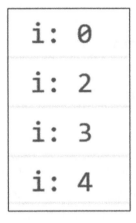

Figure 1-6. *for Loop in JavaScript*

forEach

forEach loop is called on an array or a list and executes a function for each array element. The function takes in three parameters: the current value (fruit), the index of the current value (index), and the array object that the current value belongs to. The second and third parameters are optional, whereas the first parameter is mandatory. One of the major benefits of using this control loop is that the function would not be executed for empty array elements, which results in better response time for the end application:

```
...
let fruits = ['Apple','Grapes','Watermelon'];
fruits.forEach((fruit, index) => {
    console.log(index + ': ' + fruit);
})
```

while

while loop is an entry-controlled loop similar to for loop, which means that the condition that validates the entry to the loop is checked during the beginning of the iteration. However, unlike for loop, you don't have to initialize or modify the control variable along with the condition. The initialization is done before the beginning of the loop and its value is modified in the loop body:

```
...
let fruits = ['Apple', 'Grapes', 'Watermelon'];
let i = 0;
while (i < fruits.length) {
    console.log(i + ': ' + fruits[i]);
    i++;
}
```

do...while

do...while loop is a variation of the while loop which is exit-controlled, which means that the condition that validates the entry to the loop is checked after the completion of an iteration. If true, the loop will execute the next iteration:

```
...
let fruits = ['Apple', 'Grapes', 'Watermelon'];
let i = 0;
do{
    console.log(i + ': ' + fruits[i]);
    i++;
}while (i < fruits.length);
```

The output for the forEach, while, and do...while control loop examples should be similar to that shown in Figure 1-7.

```
0: Apple
1: Grapes
2: Watermelon
```

Figure 1-7. *forEach, while, and do...while Loop in JavaScript*

There are some more variations of the forEach loop such as for...in and for...of. However, the ones listed earlier are major ones and will suffice for the scope of this chapter. Let us now look at type conversion in JavaScript.

Type Conversion

Often during programming, we need to explicitly convert member of one data type to another. This can be done by using JavaScript's built-in methods for type conversion. Consider the following example for type conversion in JavaScript:

```
...
let input = [5,9,6];
console.log("Type Of [5,9,6]: " + typeof(input));
console.log("Type Of [5,9,6]: " +
                typeof(input.toString()));
console.log("Type Of '2': " + typeof(Number('2')));
console.log("'true' to Number: " + Number(true));
console.log("'hi' to Boolean: " + Boolean('hi'));
console.log("'NaN' to Number: " + Boolean(NaN));
```

Firstly, we use toString() method which converts an object into a string. Type of a data member can be determined by passing it to the typeof() method as demonstrated in the preceding example. Then, we use the Number() method for converting string and boolean data types to numeric values. We can also convert values to boolean using the Boolean() method, which is further demonstrated in the example. Note that while doing so, values such as 0, NaN, Undefined, and so on that are empty will be converted to false, whereas all other values will be converted to true. Observe that an empty string will be converted to false, whereas a string with value "0" will be converted to true. The output of the preceding code should be similar to that shown in Figure 1-8.

```
Type Of [5,9,6]: object

Type Of [5,9,6]: string

Type Of '2': number

'true' to Number: 1

'hi' to Boolean: true

'NaN' to Boolean: false

'' to Boolean: false

'0' to Boolean: true
```

Figure 1-8. *Type Conversion in JavaScript*

That is it on type conversion. Let us now look at operators and functions in JavaScript.

Operators

Operators are used to modify the values in a program. The values we modify using operators are known as operands. JavaScript provides multiple categories of operators. Let us discuss each one of them in detail.

Arithmetic Operators

Arithmetic operators are the ones that perform mathematical operations on numeric operands. Addition (+), Subtraction (-), Multiplication (*), Division (/), Modulus (%), Increment (++), and Decrement (--) are examples of arithmetic operators.

Comparison Operators

Comparison operators compare the value of two operands and returns a boolean value based on the truthfulness of the operator. Equality (==), Type Equality (===), Inequality (!=), Greater Than (>), Greater Than or Equal To (>=), Less Than (<), and Less Than or Equal To (<=) are examples of comparison operators.

Assignment Operators

Assignment operators are used to assign values to operands. "=" operator assigns the value of right operand to the left operand, "+=" operator adds the value of right operand to left operand and assigns it to left operand, "-=" operator subtracts the value of right operand from left operand and assigns it to left operand, "∗=" operator multiplies the value of both operands and assigns it to left operand, "/=" operator divides the value of left operand to right operand and assigns it to left operand, and lastly, "%=" operand calculates the modulus after dividing left operand by right operand and assigns it to left operand.

Logical Operators

Logical operators are used to combine two or more conditions and find out their combined truthfulness. The operator returns a Boolean value. Logical AND (&&) and Logical OR (||) are two of the logical operators in JavaScript. NOT (!) is another logical operator that is used to negate the boolean value that is returned.

Ternary Operator

Ternary operator is made up of three parts: condition, body 1, and body 2. Condition and body 1 are separated by "?" operator, whereas both the bodies are separated by ":" operator. Body 1 will be executed if the condition is true, whereas body 2 will be executed if the condition is false.

Refer to the following piece of code that demonstrates all the operators in JavaScript. On executing, it should give the output similar to that shown in Figure 1-9:

```
...
var a=16, b=17;
console.log('Arithmetic Operators');
console.log('16+2 = ' + (16+2));
console.log('16-2 = ' + (16-2));
console.log('16*2 = ' + (16*2));
console.log('16/2 = ' + (16/2));
console.log('17%2 = ' + (17%2));
console.log('Comparison Operators');
console.log('1 == "1" ' + ('1' == 1));
console.log('1 === "1" ' + ('1' === 1));
console.log('1 != 2 ' + (1 != 2));
console.log('1 < 2 ' + (1 < 2));
console.log('1 > 2 ' + (1 > 2));
console.log('3 <= 3 ' + (3 <= 3));
console.log('3 >= 3 ' + (3 >= 3));
console.log('Assignment Operators');
console.log('16+=2 ' + (a+=2));
console.log('16-=2 ' + (a-=2));
console.log('16*=2 ' + (a*=2));
console.log('16/=2 ' + (a/=2));
console.log('17%=2 ' + (b%=2));
console.log('Logical Operators');
console.log('true && false: ' + (true && false));
console.log('true || false: ' + (true || false));
console.log('!true: ' + (!true));
console.log('Ternary Operator');
console.log('true?T:F --- ' + (true?'T':'F'));
```

```
Arithmetic Operators
16+2 = 18
16-2 = 14
16*2 = 32
16/2 = 8
17%2 = 1
Comparison Operators
1 == "1" true
1 === "1" false
1 != 2 true
1 < 2 true
1 > 2 false
3 <= 3 true
3 >= 3 true
Assignment Operators
16+=2 18
16-=2 16
16*=2 32
16/=2 16
17%=2 1
Logical Operators
true && false: false
true || false: true
!true: false
Ternary Operator
true?T:F --- T
```

Figure 1-9. *Operators in JavaScript*

Functions

Functions in JavaScript are self-contained pieces of code that can be written once and executed as and when required by calling or invoking the function. Functions might take in parameters and return values. However, it is not mandatory. "function" keyword is used to define a function. Given in the following is the syntax for function definition:

```
function function_name(input_paramaters)
{
     function_body
}
```

A function can also be assigned to a variable. This is known as function expression. It allows us to define anonymous functions, functions that have no name. These kinds of functions can be invoked by using the name of the variable to which they are assigned. Syntax for a function expression is as follows:

```
let variable_name = function(input_paramaters)
{
     function_body
}
```

Yet another way to define a function in JavaScript is by using arrow functions. They are similar to function expression but have a shorter syntax as follows:

```
let variable_name = (input_paramaters) =>
{
     function_body
}
```

Everything in JavaScript is done with the help of functions. For instance, when we use console.log to print values to our browser console, log() is nothing but a built-in JavaScript function that does the job for us. Consider the following example that demonstrates functions in JavaScript:

```
...
function fun()
{
    console.log('Regular JS Function.');
}
```

```
let functionExpr = function(){
    console.log('Function Expression.');
}

let arrFunction = () => {
    console.log('Arrow Function.');
}

fun();
functionExpr();
arrFunction();
```

The output in the browser console for the preceding piece of code should be similar to that shown in Figure 1-10.

```
Regular JS Function.

Function Expression.

Arrow Function.
```

Figure 1-10. *Functions in JavaScript*

Closures

Closure is an inner function having access to the scope of parent function even after the parent function has been executed. Let us understand the need of closures. Suppose that you have a counter in your program. You can use a global variable and a function to increase the value of the counter. However, the problem in this scenario is that any part of your code can modify the value of the global variable without accessing the function. To tackle this, we will need a variable that is local to the function. But if you try doing that, the variable will be initialized every time the function gets called and it will not fulfill our purpose. This is where closure comes in to the picture. Consider the following example for a better understanding:

```
...
var increment = (function () {
    var counter = 0;
```

```
    return function () {
        counter += 1;
        console.log(counter);
    }
})();
```

```
increment();
increment();
increment();
```

The result of the preceding code should be similar to that shown in Figure 1-11.

Figure 1-11. *Closures in JavaScript*

Now, let us understand what is happening here. When we assign the value of the function to the "increment" variable, the function is executed once and the entire body of the inner function is assigned to the variable because that is what the function returns. Now, when you call the function using the variable name, just the inner function will be executed. This way, the variable will remain private to the function and will be initialized just once during the assignment of function to the variable, thus fulfilling our purpose of having a private counter variable which can only be modified by invoking a designated function.

That is all about closures; let us now look at arrays in JavaScript.

Arrays

Arrays are JavaScript objects that store multiple values in single variable. You can either access a single value by specifying its index in the array or can easily iterate through all the values to find a specific value. The following is the syntax for defining an array:

```
var fruits = ['Watermelon','Apple','Grapes'];
```

We can also store other objects inside an array. For instance, consider the following example:

```
...
var fruits = ['Watermelon','Grapes'];
fruits[2] = {
            "Apple1": "Red Apple",
            "Apple2":"Green Apple"
            };
console.log(fruits);
```

The output of the preceding code should be similar to Figure 1-12.

```
                                        index.js:5
  ▼ Array(3) ⓘ
      0: "Watermelon"
      1: "Grapes"
    ▼ 2:
        Apple1: "Red Apple"
        Apple2: "Green Apple"
```

Figure 1-12. *Storing Objects in JavaScript Arrays*

Array values can be iterated over by using control loops as discussed earlier in this chapter. You can access specific array element by providing its index in the array in square brackets following the array name. You can also change its value by using assignment operator. Things will be clearer once you look at the example in the following section. You can use "length" property to get the count of array elements. Apart from this, there are several built-in array methods that you can use to perform array operations in JavaScript. The following is the list of methods:

- **arr.sort()** – This method sorts the array.

- **arr.forEach()** – This method is used to iterate over all the array elements.

- **arr.push(value)** – This method is used to add new element to the array at the last index.

- **arr.pop()** – This method removes the last value from the array.

- **arr.shift()** – This method removes the first value from the array and shifts the remaining values by one index.

- **arr.unshift(value)** – This method adds a new element to the array at the first index and shifts the remaining values by one index.

- **Array.isArray(arr)** – This method returns true if "arr" is an array.

- **arr.toString()** – This method converts an array to string of values.

- **arr.join(separator)** – This method is similar to the toString method, but you can specify a separator for the values.

- **arr1.concat(arr2)** – This method is used to concatenate two arrays: arr1 and arr2.

- **arr.splice(position, deletecount, value1, value2,...)** – This method is used to add new set of values to an array at specific position. The first parameter specifies to position at which the values need to be added, the second parameter is the count of elements to be deleted from the array, and the remaining parameters are the values that need to be added to the array.

- **arr2 = arr1.slice(firstindex, lastindex)** – This method is used to create a new array from an existing array. The parameters specify the start and end index for the values that need to be fetched for the new array. If you do not specify the lastindex, JavaScript will take all the remaining values.

Consider the following code that will help you understand the properties and methods of JavaScript arrays:

```
...
var fruits = ['Watermelon','Apple','Grapes'];
console.log('Array: ' + fruits.toString());

fruits.sort();
console.log('Sorted Array: ' + fruits.toString());
```

```
console.log('forEach:');
fruits.forEach(element => {
    console.log(element);
});

fruits.push('Strawberry');
console.log('Push: ' + fruits.toString());

fruits.pop();
console.log('Pop: ' + fruits.toString());

fruits.shift();
console.log('Shift: ' + fruits.toString());

fruits.unshift('Apple')
console.log('Unshift: ' + fruits.toString());

console.log('isArray? ' + Array.isArray(fruits));

var moreFruits = ['Strawberry'];
fruits = fruits.concat(moreFruits);
console.log('Concatenate: ' + fruits.toString());

fruits.splice(0,0,'Guava');
console.log('Splice: ' + fruits.toString());

var top3fruits = fruits.slice(0,3);
console.log('Slice: ' + top3fruits.toString());
```

The output of the preceding piece of code should be similar to Figure 1-13.

```
Array: Watermelon,Apple,Grapes
Sorted Array: Apple,Grapes,Watermelon
forEach:
Apple
Grapes
Watermelon
Push: Apple,Grapes,Watermelon,Strawberry
Pop: Apple,Grapes,Watermelon
Shift: Grapes,Watermelon
Unshift: Apple,Grapes,Watermelon
isArray? true
Concatenate: Apple,Grapes,Watermelon,Strawberry
Splice: Guava,Apple,Grapes,Watermelon,Strawberry
Slice: Guava,Apple,Grapes
```

Figure 1-13. *Arrays in JavaScript*

That is all about arrays; let us now look at arrays in classes and modules in JavaScript.

Classes and Modules

Classes in JavaScript are similar to those in other programming languages such as Java and C++. They help us create constructor functions. Modules, on the other hand, are a way to organize our code. We can break our code into multiple sections, and each section will become a separate module. Let us start with classes. We use the "class" keyword, followed by the class name to create a class in JavaScript. To instantiate an object of the class, we use the new keyword. The following is an example:

```
class Dog
{
}
let dog = new Dog();
```

Our class presently has no property or methods, so when you instantiate the class, it will create an empty object. We will now use a constructor to add some properties to our class. A constructor is a method which gets executed when an object gets created for the class. In most of the programming languages, it has the same name as the class name and does not have a return type. However, in JavaScript, a constructor is created using the "constructor" keyword. Parameters can be passed to the constructor when during the instantiation of object using new keyword. When it comes to properties, you can simply define them in the constructor using "this" keyword instead of declaring them traditionally and then defining them in the constructor. You can change the value of properties anywhere in the program with the help of assignment operator by accessing it using the object of the class. Consider the following example:

```
class Dog
{
    constructor(id){
        this.id = id;
    }
}
let dog = new Dog(100);
console.log(dog.id);
dog.id = 200;
console.log(dog.id);
```

On executing the preceding piece of code, you will get "100" and "200" as output in your browser console. We can also add method to our class to perform operations. Let us add a method that returns the value of the "id" property. Consider the following example:

```
class Dog
{
    constructor(id){
        this.id = id;
    }
}
let dog = new Dog(100);
console.log(dog.getId());
```

The preceding piece of code should print "100" to your browser console. Note that we do not need a "function" keyword while defining a method in JavaScript. We can simply use method name and go ahead with method definition. Let us now look at inheritance in JavaScript. Consider the following example:

```
class Animal
{
    constructor(type){
        this.type = type;
    }
    getType(){
        return this.type;
    }
}

class Dog extends Animal{
    constructor(){
        super('dog');
    }
}

let dog = new Dog();
console.log(dog.getType());
```

We use "extends" keyword to inherit the properties and methods of the base class in the child class. We can use "super" keyword to access members of the base class inside the child class. Outside the class, we can access members of both base class and child class using the object of the child class. The preceding piece of code should give you "dog" as output in the browser console. When we create an object of "Dog" class, its constructor gets invoked which, in turn, invokes the constructor of "Animal" class and sets the "type" property value to "dog". Then, when we try to invoke method "getType()", it searches both parent and child class for this method and invokes it if found. Note that if you do not define any constructor in the child class, the parent constructor gets invoked automatically, but if you define a constructor in the child class, you need to call the parent class constructor manually by using the "super" keyword. That is all about classes. Let us now talk about modules.

An application might have hundreds of classes. The best way to organize code for such applications is to define classes within modules. We can create a separate file for each module and then import that module in other files to use classes from that module. Let us create a "modules" folder inside "scripts" folder. In this folder, let us create a file called Animals.js. Let us now move our "Animal" class from script.js file to Animals.js file. In order to make this a module, we will need to use the "export" keyword in front of class definition. Thus, your Animals.js file should have the following code:

```
export class Animal
{
    constructor(type){
        this.type = type;
    }
    getType(){
        return this.type;
    }
}
```

However, you still cannot use this class in your index.js file. In order to do so, you will have to import the "Animal" class from Animals.js file. It can be done by using "import" keyword in your index.js file as follows:

```
import { Animal } from './modules/Animals.js';

let dog = new Animal('dog');
console.log(dog.getType());
```

You can export multiple objects from a file and import multiple objects from different files in a similar manner as shown in the preceding example. Note that in order to use modules in your project, you will also have to register the index.js script in your html file as "module" type instead of "text/JavaScript". The preceding code should ideally print "dog" in your browser console. However, if you are using chrome browser, you are bound to get an error due to CORS policy. This means that you cannot import modules from other cross-origin files without a CORS header, which is not possible if you are running your app from local file system. The solution to this problem is to run your app from a server. To do so, we will create a local server using node.js.

Creating a Local Server

The prerequisite for this is that you have Node.js and npm installed in your system. You can download and install it from `https://nodejs.org/`. Once the installation is done, you can open a terminal in your editor and make sure that the current directory is the base folder of your project. Execute the following command from the terminal:

```
npm init -y
```

This should create a "package.json" file in your project's base folder. This is a file that keeps information about your project's metadata and dependencies. Update the file to add a development server dependency and script to launch the server. The updated file should have the following information:

```
{
  "name": "intro-to-js",
  "version": "1.0.0",
  "description": "",
  "main": "index.js",
  "scripts": {
    "lite": "lite-server --port 10001",
    "start": "npm run lite"
  },
  "keywords": [],
  "author": "",
  "license": "ISC",
  "devDependencies": {
    "lite-server":"^1.3.1"
  }
}
```

After updating the "package.json" file, run the "npm install" command from the terminal to install dependency that we just added to the json file. A folder will be created in your project directory by the name "node_modules". This folder will contain files for all the project dependencies. Now that we have added a development server to our project dependency and installed it, we can launch our application using "npm start" command in the terminal. Notice that the CORS policy error that we were facing earlier during the modules example is now gone and we see "dog" as output in the browser console, as expected. This is because our application is now running on the local server and not on the file system. Notice that the URL in the browser has been changed to "localhost" from file path. Also note that the server is now listening for changes in your project files. This means that as soon as you make any changes in the project files and save it, it will automatically be reflected in the browser and you do not need to manually refresh the browser every time you change a file.

DOM Modification

DOM refers to the Document Object Model which contains all the elements in your web page. DOM can be modified using the "document" object in JavaScript. DOM is a vast topic so we will just limit our scope to selecting the elements and modifying their values. The following are the methods that can be used to select elements from DOM:

- **getElementById('elementID')** – This method returns a single element having same ID as specified in the input parameter.

- **getElementsByClassName('className')** – This method returns a list of elements having same className as specified in the input parameter. Note that unlike the getElementById method, this method can return multiple elements because ID is unique for an element whereas class name is not.

- **getElementsByTagName('tagName')** – This method returns a list of elements having same className as specified in the input parameter. Since tag name is not unique to an element, this method can return multiple elements.

Let us look at an example. I have added the following sections to the index.html file:

```
...
<h1>Introduction to JavaScript</h1>
<hr/>
<div ID="ResultContainer"></div>
<br/>
<div class="Footer">Footer Content</div>
...
```

Let us now fetch these elements using the document object methods. Consider the following JavaScript code:

```javascript
var header = document.getElementsByTagName("h1");
var body = document.getElementById("ResultContainer");
var footer = document.getElementsByClassName("Footer");

console.log(header);
console.log(body);
console.log(footer);
```

The output of the preceding piece of code should be similar to Figure 1-14.

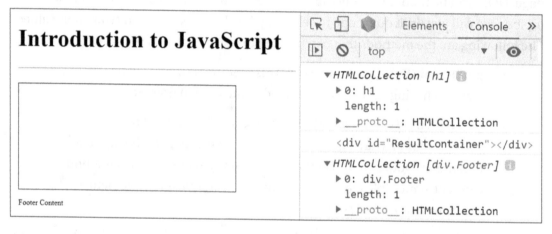

Figure 1-14. *Accessing DOM Elements in JavaScript*

Let us now modify these elements. We can change the content of these elements, add event handlers to them, and also change their visual aspects. Consider the following example:

```javascript
var header = document.getElementsByTagName("h1");
header[0].textContent = "Header Text from JS";
header[0].setAttribute('isHeader','True');
header[0].style.border = '2px solid black';
console.log(header[0]);
```

After DOM modification, your web page should look similar to Figure 1-15.

Header Text from JS

Footer Content

> Elements   Console   Sources   »
>
> top   Filter   Default   1 hidden
>
> index.js:8
> ```
> <h1 isheader="True" style="border: 2px solid black;">
> Header Text from JS</h1>
> ```

Figure 1-15. *DOM Modification in JavaScript*

Note that an attribute by the name "isheader" is added to the element and its value is set to "true". This is done with the help of setAttribute() method. Also, a border is added to the header section because of the use of style.border property in JavaScript code. There are several other properties of DOM elements that can be modified. More information can be found at https://developer.mozilla.org.

Error Handling

When something goes wrong in our JavaScript code, we would want to handle it smoothly. That is where the error handling mechanism of JavaScript comes in to the picture. Let us look at an example where the system runs into an error:

```
var fruit = new Fruit();
console.log('rest of the code!');
```

The preceding piece of code tries to instantiate "Fruit", but no such class is defined in the program. Hence, the system will run into a reference error as shown in Figure 1-16 and terminate the execution of the program. As a result, the rest of the code will not get executed.

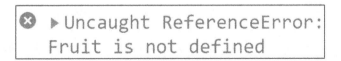

Figure 1-16. *Reference Error in JavaScript*

One of the most common ways to handle errors is to use the try-catch blocks. Error-prone code is written in the try block. If an error occurs while executing try block, the control is transferred to the following catch block which handles the execution. After the execution of catch block, the rest of the code is executed as usual. Consider the following code:

```
try{
    var fruit = new Fruit();
}
catch(e){
    console.log('ERROR: ' + e.message);
}
console.log('rest of the code!');
```

The output of this code should be similar to Figure 1-17.

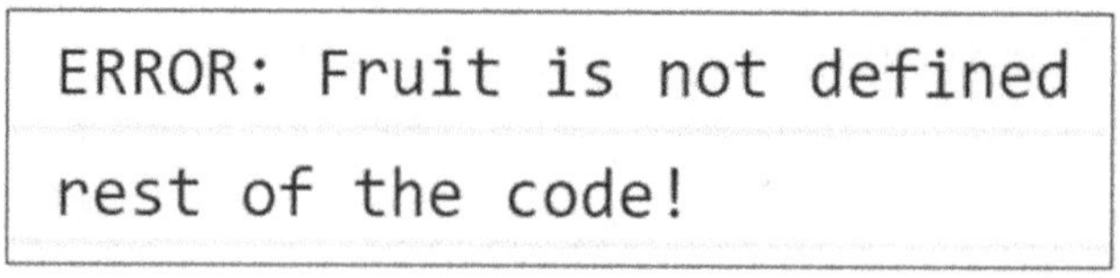

```
ERROR: Fruit is not defined
rest of the code!
```

Figure 1-17. *Error Handling in JavaScript*

Notice that despite of the error, the program does not terminate and the rest of the code gets executed as usual after error handling. A "finally" block can optionally be added after try-catch to add a piece of code that always executes regardless of the error. This is about errors that are built into JavaScript. However, as a developer, you might want to throw custom errors in certain situations. This can be done using "throw" keyword. Consider the following code:

```
...
try{
    throw new Error('Custom Developer Error!');
}
catch(e){
    console.log('ERROR: ' + e.message);
}
...
```

The preceding piece of code should print "ERROR: Custom Developer Error!" in the browser console. That is all about error handling in JavaScript. Let us now look at HTTP requests and promises.

HTTP Requests

HTTP requests in JavaScript are mostly used for fetching data and resources from a remote server or API. We will first use XMLHttpRequest(), which is JavaScript's built-in technique for HTTP requests. The following are the steps to create HTTP requests using XMLHttpRequest():

1. Instantiate an object of XMLHttpRequest().

2. Bind a function to the state change event of request object. The code in this function will monitor the request for success or failure and perform operations on the returned data.

3. Create a connection to the HTTP resource using the request object.

4. Send the request.

Consider the following example to understand it better:

```
let request = new XMLHttpRequest();

request.onreadystatechange = function(){
    if(request.readyState==4 && request.status==200){
        console.log(request.response);
    }
}

request.open('GET', 'https://api.github.com/users/msthakkar121');

request.send();
```

The output of the preceding example should be similar to Figure 1-18. Here, we use GitHub's API to get user data by specifying user's login name. We constantly monitor the request for state change using the anonymous function that is bound to the onReadyStateChange event of the request. readyState of 4 and status code of 200 means that we have successfully received response from the request. Hence, in that case we log the response object to the console. The major problem with

XMLHttpRequest() is that in order to process the response, you need to be aware of the status codes of the result for both readyState and status code. Because of this drawback, XMLHttpRequest() is rarely used directly. HTTP requests are much easier to deal with if we use a library such as JQuery.

```
{
  "login":"msthakkar121",
  "id":27701491,
  "node_id":"MDQ6VXNlcjI3NzAxNDkx",
  "avatar_url":
  "https://avatars0.githubusercontent.com/u/27701491?v=4",

  "gravatar_id":"",
  "url":"https://api.github.com/users/msthakkar121",
  "html_url":
  "https://github.com/msthakkar121",
  "followers_url":
  "https://api.github.com/users/msthakkar121/followers",

  "following_url":
  "https://api.github.com/users/msthakkar121/following{/other_user}",

  "gists_url":"https://api.github.com/users/msthakkar121/gists{/gist_id}",

  "starred_url":
  "https://api.github.com/users/msthakkar121/starred{/owner}{/repo}",

  "subscriptions_url":
  "https://api.github.com/users/msthakkar121/subscriptions",

  "organizations_url":"https://api.github.com/users/msthakkar121/orgs",
  "repos_url":
  "https://api.github.com/users/msthakkar121/repos",
  "events_url":
  "https://api.github.com/users/msthakkar121/events{/privacy}",

  "received_events_url":
  "https://api.github.com/users/msthakkar121/received_events",
  "type":
  "User",
  "site_admin":false,
  "name": "MohitThakkar",
  "company":null,
  "blog":"",
  "location":null,
  "email":null,
  "hireabl...
```

Figure 1-18. *XMLHttpRequest in JavaScript*

Let us look at HTTP requests using JQuery. To use JQuery in our project, we will have to first register it in "package.json" file and install it in the "node_modules" folder of our project. Both of these can be done by executing the "npm install jquery" command from the terminal. Once we install JQuery to our project, we can import it in our JavaScript file using the import statement. Consider the following example:

```
import '../node_modules/jquery/dist/jquery.js';

$.get("https://api.github.com/users/msthakkar121", data => console.log(data));
```

"$" symbol is a constant in JQuery and is defined as static. We use this symbol to access the get method. The first parameter to this method is a string containing the URL to which the request is being sent. The second parameter is a function that will be executed if the request succeeds. The third parameter is optional and might contain data that needs to be sent along with the request. In the preceding example, we have used an arrow function that will log the response data to the browser console. The output of the preceding code should be similar to Figure 1-18. Even though this seems like a good way to deal with HTTP requests, it is not the ideal way. The get() method returns a promise which helps us work with the request in a much better way.

Promises

Promises are designed to work with asynchronous requests. They are objects that store the response of asynchronous requests. Consider the following piece of code:

```
let promise = new Promise(function(resolve, reject){
    setTimeout(resolve,100,'Resolved');
    //setTimeout(reject,100,'Rejected');
});

promise.then(
    value => console.log('Success: ' + value),
    error => console.log('Error: ' + error)
);
```

Promise constructor takes in a function with two arguments. These two arguments are again functions that are called for success and failure, respectively. In the preceding example, we create promise with an anonymous function. This function has two arguments: resolve and reject. In the body of the anonymous function, we are calling "resolve" function with a timeout of 100 milliseconds and passing "Resolved" as a value to the promise. Thus, the promise will be in success state and will store the message that we passed as a response. If we call "reject" function instead of resolve, the promise will be in error state.

That is all about creating a promise. Now, consider the scenario where you want to perform some operation based on success or failure of a promise. In that case, you will have to settle a promise using then() function. then() is a function in the promise object that takes in two arguments. The first argument is a function with one parameter which gets executed when the promise is in success state. The second argument is a function with one parameter which gets executed when the promise is in failure state. The parameter of these functions will contain the value that was returned during the resolution of the promise.

In the preceding piece of code, if you resolved the promise, the output on your browser console should be "Success: Resolved", and if you rejected the promise, it should be "Error: Rejected". Note that you might have to wait for a while before the promise is settled because you will be dealing with asynchronous operations here.

Let us now look at the example that we were working on in the previous section ("HTTP Requests"):

```
$.get("https://api.github.com/users/msthakkar121", data => console.log(data));
```

The preceding piece of code can be rewritten using promise as follows:

```
let promise = $.get("https://api.github.com/users/msthakkar100");

promise.then(
    data => console.log(data),
    error => console.log(error)
);
```

That is all about promises. With the end of this topic, we also come to the end of this chapter. In the next chapter, we will use the JavaScript concepts that we learned so far in order to learn about React.js, a JavaScript-based library.

Summary

- JavaScript is the most important language for web development, and it is necessary to create applications that run on web browsers.

- Constants are identifiers in JavaScript whose values remain same throughout the program, whereas variables are identifiers whose values are prone to change.

- Variables are defined using either "let" or "var" keyword. It is recommended to use "let" keyword because variables defined using "let" are scoped and strictly checked for inappropriate usage.

- Rest parameter helps us club multiple function input parameters into a single array. On the other hand, spread syntax is the exact opposite of rest parameter and helps us destructure an input array into multiple variables.

- Control loops such as for, forEach, while, and do...while are used to work with iterations in JavaScript.

- Type conversion is a provision built in JavaScript that can be used to explicitly convert member of one data type to another.

- Various arithmetic, comparison, assignment, logical, and ternary operators are provided in JavaScript that can be used to modify the values of operands.

- Functions are pieces of code that can be written once and utilized multiple times in a program.

- Classes and modules help us get the essence of object-oriented programming in JavaScript. Modules help us organize our code into files and share the code across the project using export and import keywords.

- We can access and modify HTML elements of our web page using JavaScript's document object.

- Errors in JavaScript can be handled using try-catch block. "finally" block can also be used optionally. Custom errors can be generated using the "throw" keyword.

- XML http requests can be used to fetch data from remote server or APIs. However, get() method of JQuery library is much more convenient to do so.

- While working with asynchronous requests, promises can be used to conveniently deal with success and error states of the response.

CHAPTER 2

Introducing React.js

React.js is an open source JavaScript library created by Facebook in May 2013. It is used for building user interfaces. The best part about React is that it uses a declarative style of programming rather than an imperative style. While the former one specifies the compiler what to do, the latter one also has to specify how to do it. Thus, programming with React results in less code.

In this chapter, we will understand the underlying principles of React, one at a time. We will also see how each principle works in practice. If you have studied the previous chapter, this chapter should not be difficult to comprehend. If you have not, I recommend you to once go through the previous chapter.

Setting Up the Environment

In order to start programming with React, I'll be using the Visual Studio Code editor which can be downloaded from `https://code.visualstudio.com/download`. However, you can use any editor of your choice.

Installing Node.js

Node.js is an open source, cross-platform runtime environment that helps us write JavaScript applications and execute it. We installed node.js during the previous chapter while we created a local server for working with cross-origin requests for module imports in JavaScript. If you have not yet installed node.js, you can download and install it from `https://nodejs.org/`. Once it is installed, you can open a terminal in your editor and run "node -v" command to check if the node.js has installed correctly. If yes, the terminal will display the installed version number of node.js.

© Mohit Thakkar 2020
M. Thakkar, *Building React Apps with Server-Side Rendering*, https://doi.org/10.1007/978-1-4842-5869-9_2

Node.js runtime has thousands of modules that are readily available for use. These modules are nothing but pre-written JavaScript applications that can be reused in your code. These modules can be added to your code using npm (Node Package Manager). npm is shipped along with node.js and should already be installed in your system if you have installed node.js. You can execute "npm -v" command in the terminal. If installed correctly, this command will display the version of npm installed in your system.

Installing React

In order to use react, you must first install it to your project. There are multiple ways of doing this. One way is to simply add the js files to your HTML template using <script> tag as follows:

```
<script src="https://unpkg.com/react@16/umd/react.development.js" crossorigin>
</script>

  <script src="https://unpkg.com/react-dom@16/umd/react-dom.development.js"
  crossorigin></script>
```

Note that the preceding files are the development versions and you will have to use minified, production versions for enhanced performance in a production environment. The following are the minified versions:

```
<script src="https://unpkg.com/react@16/umd/react.production.min.js"
crossorigin></script>

<script src="https://unpkg.com/react-dom@16/umd/react-dom.production.min.js"
crossorigin></script>
```

Another way is to manually create a folder for your project and add a "package.json" file with a list of all the dependencies. You can then use the "npm-install" command to install all the dependencies into the "node_modules" folder in your project folder. Once the dependencies are installed, you can start referencing the dependencies in your JavaScript and HTML files.

However, there is a much better way to get started with a React project. We will use "create-react-app", an existing react node module for beginners. Within the terminal, you can navigate to the directory you want to create your application in and execute the following command:

```
npx create-react-app my-app
```

Note that we have used npx instead of npm. npx is Node Package Runner that comes with npm version 5.2 and higher. While npm is used to install packages, npx is used to execute packages. In this case, we are not actually installing the "create-react-app" package on our system, but we are executing that package, which, in turn, will install a react application on our system. If you use npm, you will have to first install the "create-react-app" package to your system using the following command:

```
npm install create-react-app
```

And then, use that package to create a react application using the following command:

```
create-react-app my-app
```

Thus, we will simply use npx instead of npm. On successful execution of the command, you should see output similar to the following:

```
C:\Users\Mohit.Thakkar\...\Chapter_02> npx create-react-app my-app

npx: installed 91 in 35.563s

Creating a new React app in C:\Users\Mohit.Thakkar\...\Chapter_02\my-app.

Installing packages. This might take a couple of minutes.

Installing react, react-dom, and react-scripts...

> core-js@2.6.10 postinstall C:\Users\Mohit.Thakkar\...\Chapter_02\my-app\
node_modules\babel-runtime\node_modules\core-js

> node postinstall || echo "ignore"

> core-js@3.2.1 postinstall C:\Users\Mohit.Thakkar\...\my-app\node_modules\
core-js

> node scripts/postinstall || echo "ignore"

+ react-dom@16.12.0
+ react-scripts@3.2.0
+ react@16.12.0

added 1475 packages from 693 contributors and audited 904933 packages in
264.267s
found 0 vulnerabilities
```

Success! Created my-app at C:\Users\Mohit.Thakkar\...\Chapter_02\my-app

Inside that directory, you can run several commands:

  npm start
    Starts the development server.

  npm run build
    Bundles the app into static files for production.

  npm test
    Starts the test runner.

  npm run eject
    Removes this tool and copies build dependencies, configuration files
and scripts into the app directory. If you do this, you can't go back!

We suggest that you begin by typing:

  cd my-app
  npm start

Happy hacking!

If you navigate to the my-app folder and open the package.json file, you will
notice that your project has dependencies on react, react-dom, and react-scripts. You
can add more dependencies to this list as and when required. Let us now launch this
application using the "npm start" command in the terminal. Make sure to change
your directory in the terminal to the "my-app" folder. You will notice that the app
will run on a local development server on port 3000. You will see an output similar to
Figure 2-1.

Figure 2-1. *create-react-app*

If you look at the file explorer, you will see an "index.html" file in the "public" folder and lots of .js files in the "src" folder. These JavaScript files are the true essence of react. They create components and render them on the browser. Since we are going to learn about react components one by one, we can delete all the files in the "src" folder for now. Note that as soon as you delete the files, you will start getting a not-found error for the "index.js" file. This is because "create-react-app" has a dependency on react-scripts which uses a webpack configuration file to specify an entry point for the application as "index.js". So when we delete the files, it will no longer be able to find an entry point into the application and will throw an error. To resolve this error, we will add an empty "index.js" file for now. If you look at the browser screen after adding the file, you will notice that the output will be a blank window but there will be no errors.

Basic Concepts of React

Components are a major backbone of React. They are similar to functions, take in props (input), output UI elements, and can be reused as and when required in other files. Even though they are similar to functions, you need not invoke them. They can be used like HTML elements (<ComponentName/>).

45

Its reactive nature is another important concept in React. This relates to data binding. Data in a react component comes from props, which are component input. When this data changes, the UI changes as well. This is handled automatically by React.

Another great concept of React is that HTML is generated using JavaScript. And this is justified because when your application receives data from the server, you need to process that data before presenting it. You can either use HTML to do this or you can use JavaScript, which is a way better option. Now that you are using JavaScript to process the data, you might as well present it using JavaScript. That's exactly what React does.

This brings us to the next concept of React: the virtual DOM. Since HTML is generated using JavaScript, React would not have access to the DOM before it is generated; hence, it keeps a virtual representation of the views and then uses it to compare the changes in UI.

Let us now look at some more concepts of React which are necessary to understand in order to build a React application.

Single-Page Applications

Traditionally, when your application contains multiple pages and you click a link to navigate to another page, a new request is sent to the server and the browser then loads the new page when a response is received from the server. This process is very time- and resource-consuming. It can be improved with the implementation of single-page applications (SPAs). This is something popularized by client-side rendering provided by JavaScript frameworks such as React. In SPAs, you only load the page once. Later on, when the user requests a new page, JavaScript interprets the request, asynchronously gets data from the server, fetches the UI component that needs to be updated, and updates the section of the page with new data without reloading the entire page.

Due to the asynchronous nature of such requests, the user might have to wait for a while before the UI changes. However, user experience can be enhanced by using attractive loaders. A major benefit of SPAs is that resources that remain constant throughout the application (such as stylesheets and scripts) need not be reloaded every time a request is made, resulting in quicker response time. However, search engines have trouble indexing the SPAs. This is why if your application needs indexing, relying entirely on client-side rendering is not a good idea. Another point that you need to keep in mind is that unlike most server-side programming languages, JavaScript does not have a built-in mechanism to handle memory leaks. It is your responsibility to take care of memory issues because if existent, they might exhaust the browser memory and significantly decrease the speed of your application. In the later part of this book, we will see how to tackle these issues by implementing server-side rendering in React applications.

Immutability

Immutability is the property of an object, due to which you cannot change its value once it is defined. In order to modify the value of such objects, you have to create a new object and assign it to the same name. Immutability is seen in React in many places. For example, the state object in React which is passed as a function input is never modified directly. Its value is altered only through the setState() method. This is necessary in React in order to track changes in the state of a component. As discussed earlier, React compares the virtual DOM with the older version to see what values are changed and subsequently update only those sections in the UI that needs updating. This is known as the reconciliation process. To check if the state has changed, you have to implement the following method in React:

```
shouldComponentUpdate(nextProps, nextState) {
  if(this.props.myProp !== nextProps.myProp) {
    return true;
  }
  return false;
}
```

If the method returns true, React will update the UI for the component. If the state object is mutable, the value of "this.props.myProp" will immediately be modified when the state changes and there will be no trace of previous value to compare. Since the state object is immutable, a new object (nextProps) will be created when you modify the state which will hold the new value. Due to this, React can easily compare new values with the old ones before updating the UI.

Note that immutability has some disadvantages as well. For example, you have to make sure that you use methods like setState() to modify objects like the state object in React. If not used carefully, Immutability might hurt the performance of your application.

Purity

In computer science, purity refers to the ability of a function to always return the same value for the same set of input parameters without causing any side effects or external modification. A pure function never modifies the values of input parameters. It rather returns a new object every time it is invoked. Consider the following example for a pure function:

```
function add(a, b) {
  return a + b;
}
```

No matter how many times you call this function, it will always return the sum of parameters. Now consider the following example for an impure function:

```
function GetTodayDate() {
  const date = new Date();
  return date;
}
```

The output of the preceding function depends on time and, hence, will be different every time you invoke it. These kinds of functions are impure functions. Not all functions can be pure. Sometimes, you might want to get some inputs from the outside world or make some changes to the external environment. In such cases, we use impure functions.

In React, a component is referred to as a pure component if its output depends only on its props (function inputs). If the state of the component is involved in computing its output, the component is said to be impure.

Composition

In React, composition refers to a pattern of how components are created using props. It allows us to have several advantages such as creating specialized versions of a common component, pass a method as props, and use props.children property to pass on components to other components. Consider the following example:

```
const GenericButton = props => {
  return <button> {props.text} </button>
}
```

```
const ResetButton = () => {
  return <GenericButton text="Reset"/>
}
```

In the preceding example, we are creating a generic button component whose text will differ based on the prop it receives. Furthermore, we are creating a reset button component that will call the generic button component with the text property "Reset". In a similar manner, we can also create other kinds of buttons such as login button, submit button, and so on. Consider the following example that demonstrates how to pass a method as props:

```
const GenericButton = props => {
  return <button onClick={props.onClickHandler}>
          {props.text}
        </button>
}

const ResetButton = () => {

  const onClickHandler = () => {
    alert('reset button clicked')
  }

  return <GenericButton text="Reset"
            onClickHandler={onClickHandler}/>
}
```

The preceding example is similar to the previous one. The only difference is that we are creating a method inside the reset button component for the click event and passing it along with the props. This method can be used inside the generic button component. Now let us consider the following example that demonstrates the use of props.children property:

```
const GenericButton = props => {
  return <div>
          <button> {props.text} </button>
          {props.children}
        </div>
}
```

```
const ResetButton = () => {
  return <GenericButton text="Reset">
          <p>Click to reset text.</p>
        </GenericButton>
}
```

In the preceding example, we are passing a paragraph tag while rendering the generic button component. We are not passing this as a property inside the props. So the question is where will props store it? React has a simple explanation for this. Anything written between the opening and closing tag of a component is stored in a special property: props.children. One thing to note is that simply passing the children elements while invoking the component is not enough. React will only render the children elements if we have used a placeholder for the props.children property. That's it about composition in React. If the picture is a bit blurry to you right now, don't worry. Things will get clear as we move forward into the chapter. Let us now look at component types in React.

Creating Your First React Component

When we installed React to our project using the "create-react-app" command at the beginning of this chapter, it created multiple JavaScript files under the "src" folder for our project, most of which we deleted. We also cleaned up the index.js file which was the starting point of our application. We will create a new JavaScript file for our component in the "src" folder. We will then import this component in index.js file and render the newly created component. We will create a component with an input box, a button, and a label. On the press of a button, the component should override the label text with the text in the input box.

To do this, we will have to render these elements to the browser. As discussed earlier, React renders HTML to the browser using JavaScript. We will see two different approaches to do this – one using JavaScript and the other using JSX.

Creating Elements Using JavaScript

While using JavaScript, we use two major methods to create and render a component – createElement() and render().

createElement() is a method provided by React which takes in three arguments. The following is the method signature:

```
React.createElement(
  type, [props], [...children]
)
```

- The "type" argument can either be a tag name such as "div" or "p" or it can be a React component.

- The "props" argument can be used to specify any property values such as "id" or "name" for the element in the form of a JavaScript object.

- The "...children" argument specifies the child elements of the element that we are creating. It can be in the form of a number, text, or another React element.

Consider the following piece of code that will create a paragraph element:

```
React.createElement(
                    'p',
                    {id: 'para1'},
                    'Hello from React'
                );
```

React will compile the preceding code and create the following HTML equivalent:

```
<p id="para1">Hello from React</p>
```

Now that we have created the element, we would want to render it on the browser. To do so, we will use the render() method provided by "react-dom" library. The following is the method signature:

```
ReactDOM.render(element, container)
```

51

- The "element" argument is the element that you created using the React.createElement() method. You can store the output of the createElement() method in a variable and pass it as the "element" argument.

- The "container" argument is the parent element within which you wish to render the current element. You can use JavaScript's document.getElementById(), document.getElementsByClassName(), or document.getElementsByTagName() to fetch the parent element and pass it as "container" argument.

Add the following piece of code to your index.js file in order to create and render an element using the JavaScript approach:

```
import React from 'react';
import ReactDOM from 'react-dom';

var reactElement = React.createElement(
    'p',
    {id: 'para1'},
    'Hello from React'
);

ReactDOM.render(reactElement, document.getElementBy('root'));
```

We first import the React and ReactDOM modules from the libraries (something we came across during the "Classes and Modules" section in the previous chapter). Then we create a paragraph element using the createElement() method and, finally, render it using the render() method. Note that we already have a "div" element in our index. html file with "root" as id. Thus, we are using the same as a parent element to render the paragraph that we created. If you run the code in the browser, you should see an output similar to Figure 2-2.

Hello from React

Figure 2-2. *Creating Elements Using JavaScript and JSX*

If you inspect the browser window and check the source, you shall find the following HTML code:

```
<div id="root">
 <p id="para1">Hello from React</p>
</div>
```

Now that you are familiar with the JavaScript approach of creating and rendering elements, let us look at a better approach.

Creating Elements Using JSX

Creating HTML elements using the JavaScript approach significantly reduces the readability of the code, especially when you are creating a large number of elements. JSX is an HTML-like syntax in JavaScript which allows us to create HTML elements without invoking the React.createElement() method. However, in the background, what happens is that the JSX elements automatically get compiled to the createElement() method calls. The major benefit of using JSX is that it significantly enhances code readability and allows developers to write structured code. To render the JSX elements, we use the same render() method provided by ReactDOM. Let us look at the following code to understand the JSX approach to create the same paragraph tag that we created in the previous example:

```
import React from 'react';
import ReactDOM from 'react-dom';

const ParaText = 'Hello from React';
const reactElement = <p id='para1'>{ParaText}</p>

ReactDOM.render(reactElement, document.getElementById('root'));
```

Executing the preceding code in browser, you would get a similar output to Figure 2-2 and the following HTML equivalent will be generated:

```
<div id="root">
 <p id="para1">Hello from React</p>
</div>
```

As you see, the JSX approach gives us the same output as the JavaScript approach but has a way better developer experience. Thus, we will use JSX to create our first react component.

Function vs. Class Component

There are two ways you can create a component in React – one using functions and another using class. A major difference between the two is the syntax. Function components are created using plain JavaScript functions that take in props as an input parameter and return a react component. On the other hand, class components are created using JavaScript class syntax and need to extend from React.Component class. A major benefit of using class components is that you can use React's state object which is provided by React.Component class. Since function components are plain JavaScript functions, you cannot use the state object in function components. We will learn about the concept of state later in the chapter.

Let us get back to our initial plan of creating a component with an input box, a button, and a label. Create a file "MyComponent.js" under the "src" folder. Add the following code to the file:

```
import React from 'react';

function MyComponent(){
    return(
        <div>
            <input id='inputTextbox'></input>
            <button type='submit'
                onClick={UpdateText}>
                Update
            </button>
            <br/>
            <label id='output'></label>
        </div>
    );
}

function UpdateText(){
    document.getElementById('output').innerText = document.
getElementById('inputTextbox').value;
}

export default MyComponent;
```

The preceding code is the function approach of creating the component that we needed. It is created as a separate module by the name "MyComponent" and is exported. We have also created a function "UpdateText()" which contains the logic to update the label value on button click. We have passed this function as props to the button element using JSX syntax. React automatically binds it to the onClick event of the button. Now let us look at the class approach of creating the same component. Consider the following code that will go in your "MyComponent.js" file:

```
import React from 'react';

class MyComponent extends React.Component{

    UpdateText(){
        document.getElementById('output').innerText = document.
getElementById('inputTextbox').value;
    }

    render(){
        return(
        <div>
            <input id='inputTextbox'></input>
            <button type='button'
                onClick={this.UpdateText}>
                Update
            </button>
            <br/>
            <label id='output'></label>
        </div>
        );
    }
}

export default MyComponent;
```

The preceding code represents the class approach of creating a component. It will give us the same output as the function approach we saw earlier. In this approach, we define functions as a member of the class and we use "this" keyword to access those functions within the class. The same is observed when we pass the "UpdateText()"

function as props for the "onClick" event of the button. React.Component class provides the "render()" method which we override in order to write our JSX code that the component will return. Let us now import this module in index.js file and render this component to the browser. Add the following code to your index.js file:

```
import React from 'react';
import ReactDOM from 'react-dom';
import MyComponent from './MyComponent';

ReactDOM.render(<MyComponent/>, document.getElementById('root'));
```

That is it. We have just created our first react component. If you execute the preceding code in the browser, you would see a textbox and a button similar to Figure 2-3. On button click, the value of the textbox will be copied to the label below.

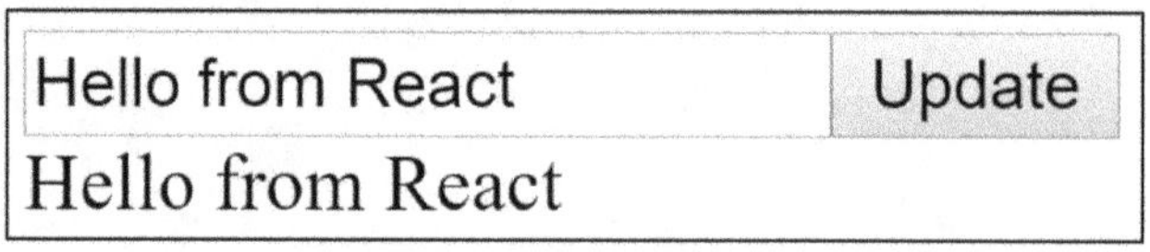

Figure 2-3. *First React Component*

Passing Props

Props are nothing but values that are passed to React components with the help of HTML attributes while invoking them using JSX. Passing props is not necessary unless you are using them in the component. However, React recommends that you always pass props in order to ensure compatibility with future changes. Props that are passed to a component can be accessed using "this.props.propName" syntax. One thing to note is that if you are using class syntax to create a component and you have defined a constructor function, it is always advisable to pass props to the constructor function as well as React.Component class via super() method. Consider the following example:

MyComponent.js

```
import React from 'react';

class MyComponent extends React.Component{

    render(){
        return(
```

```
    <div>
        <label>{this.props.text}</label>
    </div>
    );
  }
}

export default MyComponent;
```

Index.js

```
import React from 'react';
import ReactDOM from 'react-dom';
import MyComponent from './MyComponent';

ReactDOM.render(<MyComponent text='Hello from React'/>, document.
getElementById('root'));
```

Note   React props are read-only and you will not be able to modify their value.

In the preceding example, we are passing a simple string as props and displaying it on a label, but you can also pass variables and objects by wrapping them in curly brackets.

Stateless and Stateful React Components

So far, we have learned how to create react components using JSX and render it to the browser. This is enough to create static web sites. However, React is well known for the creation of user interactive interfaces, one that reacts to user events. To build such interfaces, it is necessary to understand how React manages state. Now, you might wonder that we already built a react application that reacts to the user's button click event in order to update a label. We did this using JavaScript's built-in event handler. React, on the other hand, has a better way of managing this, which is by using state.

State is an object that contains a set of properties that controls the behavior of the component. The values of these properties might change over the lifetime of the component. Instead of re-rendering the entire view every time some value changes, we can store this value inside the state object, and whenever the state object gets updated, React will partially update the view. The components that use the state object are Stateful components and the ones that do not are Stateless components. As discussed earlier, since state object is available by extending from React.Component class, it can only be used in class components and not in function components.

Presentational vs. Container Components   Note that Stateless components are also known by the name Presentational components and Stateful components as Container components.

Working with the State Object

Let us see an example of how to work with the "state" object. Consider the following piece of code that will go in your MyComponent.js file. Feel free to create a separate component but do remember to import it in your index.js file before using it:

```
import React from 'react';

class MyComponent extends React.Component{

  constructor(props){
    super(props);
    this.state = {outputText: 'Placeholder'};
  }

  UpdateText = () => {
    this.setState({
      outputText: document.getElementById('inputTextbox').value
    });
  }

  render(){
    return(
      <div>
        <input id='inputTextbox' type='text'></input>
        <button type='button'
```

```
            onClick={this.UpdateText}>
            Update
        </button>
        <br/>
        <label id='output'>
          {this.state.outputText}
        </label>
      </div>
    );
  }
}

export default MyComponent;
```

The output of the preceding code should be similar to Figure 2-3. We are doing the same thing that we did in our first React application. We have a textbox, a label, and a button. On the click of the button, the text entered in the textbox should reflect on the label. However, the major difference here is that we are using React's built-in state object to store the initial label value, and instead of directly updating the label, we will update the state object while React will handle the changes in the view.

We have initialized the state object in our class constructor. Note that we have extended the React.Component class to our class. This is where the state object comes from. Before initializing the state object in the constructor, it is necessary to call the super() method that will allow us to access members of the React.Component class in our class. The JSX code that the component returns is the same as the one that we wrote earlier while creating our first React app. The only difference is that the value of the label is now bound to the state object property using the curly braces. Doing this helps React in understanding that it needs to change the value of the label when the state object changes.

Note   While working with the state object, keep in mind that it is case-sensitive. So, if you write "State" instead of "state", React will consider it as a normal JavaScript object instead of the built-in state object.

The other difference that you will notice is in the UpdateText() method which executes on the click event of the button. Instead of directly updating the label, unlike last time, we now use the setState() method to update the property value of the state object. The setState() method is provided by the React.Component class to modify the state object and can be accessed using "this" keyword. When the state changes, React will automatically update the label value in the view. This is the benefit of using the state object.

Note   You should always use the setState() method while modifying the state object instead of directly updating the value using the assignment operator. Because when this method is called, React compares the new virtual DOM with the existing one and makes necessary changes to the UI. If you directly update the values using the assignment operator, React will never know about the changes in the virtual DOM and it will not be reflected on the UI.

One of the major benefits of using state is that it enables the creation of interactive components. For instance, if a user is interacting with one particular component on a screen with multiple components, react will only make changes to that particular component and the other components will completely be isolated to those changes.

Another thing to know about the state object is that it is immutable. So, when you modify the value of the state object using the setState() method, a new copy of the object is created. This allows a comparison between the previous state and the new state. That is how React keeps track of changes and updates the UI.

Even though the state object is similar to the props object, a significant difference between the two is that unlike props object, the state object is private to a component and is completely controlled by the component. When you pass down props to a component, it cannot modify them because they are read-only. But in the case of the state object, the component has the complete liberty to make any kind of changes.

Despite all these benefits, one might opt against using the state object. It is up to you to decide whether you want to build a stateful component or a presentational component. That is it about the state object. Let us now look at the lifecycle of a React component.

React Lifecycle

Every component in React goes through certain lifecycle methods. You can override these methods in your code in order to implement certain functionalities in your application. But before doing so, it is necessary to understand the lifecycle of a React component. Figure 2-4 shows the lifecycle diagram of a React component.

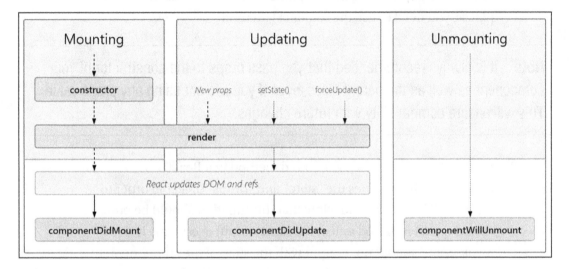

Figure 2-4. *The Lifecycle of a React Component*

The three major phases of the React component lifecycle are mounting, updating, and unmounting.

Mounting

Mounting is the process of creating an instance of a React component and inserting it into the DOM. When a component is mounted, the following methods are invoked in the respective order:

1. **constructor(props)** – The constructor is the first method that is called when a component is instantiated. This is the place where the initial state of the component is set and methods are bound. If you do not have to initialize the state and bind any methods, you do not need to implement a constructor for your component. However, if you do implement the constructor, the first thing that

you always need to do is call the parent constructor from your constructor using the super(props) method. This will allow your component to inherit the properties of React.Component class. If you do not do this, then you will not be able to access "this.props" object in your constructor. One important thing to note is that the constructor is the only place where you can directly assign value to the state object using the assignment operator. At all other places, you need to use the setState() method.

Note   It is always recommended that you pass props to the constructor of your component as well as the parent class, even if you are not using any props value. This will ensure compatibility with future changes.

---

2. **render()** – This is the only required method in a React component. It examines the "state" and "props" object in order to return HTML to the DOM. Note that this function should be pure, meaning that it should return the same output every time it is invoked and should not tamper with the state of the component. If you need to perform operations that might modify the component state, such code should be written in componentDidMount() method instead.

3. **componentDidMount()** – This method is invoked immediately after a component is mounted to the DOM tree. The operations that require the elements to be present on the DOM should be performed here. For instance, if you need to load data from a remote resource, this method would be a good place to initiate a network request. If your component needs to subscribe to some events, you can write that code here. However, make sure that you do not forget to unsubscribe the subscriptions in the componentWillUnmount() method. Also, if you want to update the state of the component, setState() method should be invoked from here.

Updating

A component is re-rendered whenever there is a change in its "props" or "state" object. If your component has certain dependencies, you can also tell React to forcefully re-render it by calling the forceUpdate() method. Under all scenarios, the following methods are called when a component is updated:

1. **getDerivedStateFromProps(props, state)** – This is the first method to be invoked when a component gets updated. If the state needs to be updated, this method should return an object, else it should return null. This method is used in scenarios where the state needs to be updated depending on the updates to the props object.

2. **shouldComponentUpdate(nextProps, nextState)** – This method returns a Boolean value to let React know whether the view should be re-rendered. It returns "True" by default so React will re-render the view on every state change. You can use this method for performance optimization. Whether or not the view needs updating can be decided manually by comparing this.props with nextProps and this.state with nextState.

3. **render()** – This is the same as the one that is called when a component is mounted for the first time. However, in this case, render() method will not be invoked if shouldComponentUpdate() method returns "False".

4. **getSnapshotBeforeUpdate(prevProps, prevState)** – This method is invoked just before the updated values are committed to the DOM tree. It gives us a chance to capture any information related to the current state of the component. The value returned by this method will be passed as a parameter to the componentDidUpdate() method.

5. **componentDidUpdate(prevProps, prevState, snapshot)** – This method is invoked immediately after the DOM has been updated. It will not be invoked if shouldComponentUpdate() method returns "False". This is a good place to initiate a network request if necessary. For instance, you might want to post the updated data

values to some remote data server. To do so, you can compare prevProps with this.props to determine whether the values have changed and initiate a POST request depending on the result of the comparison.

Unmounting

This is the last phase of the React component lifecycle. It is in this phase that the component is removed (unmounted) from the DOM. React has just one method that gets invoked during the unmounting.

1. **componentWillUnmount()** – This method is invoked just before the component is about to be removed from the DOM tree. This is a good place to perform cleanup operations. For instance, you might want to unsubscribe from any events that the component subscribed to during componentDidMount() method or cancel any network requests that are in the pipeline.

Now that you have a thorough understanding of the lifecycle of React components, let us study about Hooks in React.

Hooks

We have discussed earlier in this chapter that there are certain functionalities, such as state object and lifecycle methods, provided by React.Component class which can only be used within class components. With the introduction of Hooks in React 16.8, this is no longer the case.

Hooks are React functions that let us hook into the React state and lifecycle features from within the function components, hence eliminating the need for using the class approach to build stateful React components. You need to adhere to the following two rules while using Hooks in React:

- Don't call Hooks inside loops, conditions, or nested functions. Only call Hooks at the top level of your function component.

- Don't call Hooks from regular JavaScript functions. Only call them from React function components or custom Hooks.

Note   Hooks do not work inside class components. They can only be used within function components.

React provides a few built-in hooks to start with. However, developers can write their own custom hooks and use them in their applications. In the following section, we will learn about the two of the most used React hooks – State Hook and Effect Hook, both of which comes built in to React.

State Hook

React library provides a function called "useState()" which can be invoked inside a function component to add stateful behavior. useState() returns a state value and a function that can be used to update the state value. It takes in the initial state value as an input parameter. Let us consider the same example that we saw earlier – the one with an input box, a button, and a label. We will set the initial value of the label to "Placeholder" and will update it with text in the input box on button click. We will use the useState() method to define a state variable that will store the label value and a method that will update the state value. Consider the following piece of code that will go in your MyComponent.js file:

```
import React, {useState} from 'react';

function MyComponent(props){

 const [outputValue, setOutputValue] =
 useState('Placeholder');

 function UpdateText(){
   setOutputValue(
     document.getElementById('inputTextbox').value
   );
 }

 return(
   <div>
     <input id='inputTextbox'></input>
     <button type='button'
```

```
        onClick={UpdateText}>
        Update
    </button>
    <br/>
    <label>{outputValue}</label>
  </div>
 );
}

export default MyComponent;
```

When you render this component using ReactDOM.render() method in your index. js file, you should get browser output similar to Figure 2-3. We first import the useState() method from the React library, then we declare constants "outputValue", which will store the label text, and "setOutputValue", which will be the method that updates the state. To get the values for these two constants, we invoke the useState() method with initial value as an input parameter.

We invoke the setOutputValue() method with the new value as an input parameter whenever we want to update the state value, in this case, on button click.

You will notice that we have not manually updated the view from the code. We have just updated the value of our state object. It is important to note that this is a function component and we are not extending the Component class. Despite this, we are able to use the state object provided by the Component class and React automatically re-renders the view as soon as the state object is modified. This is the power of State Hook provided by React. Let us now look at one more built-in Hook in React that is widely used.

Effect Hook

Effect Hook lets you perform side effects in a function component. This means that if you want to perform some operations based on the lifecycle events of a react component, Effect Hook is the ideal one to use.

Operations such as initiating a network request for data, subscribing to events, and manually updating the DOM are known as side effects because such operations might affect other components and cannot be performed during rendering.

The useEffect() method from React library helps us implement the Effect Hook. It is similar to componentDidMount(), componentDidUpdate(), and componentWillUnmount() methods of React classes. Let us look at the following example to have a better understanding:

```
import React, {useState, useEffect} from 'react';

function MyComponent(props){

 const [outputValue, setOutputValue] =
 useState('Placeholder');

 function UpdateText(){
   setOutputValue(
     document.getElementById('inputTextbox').value
   );
 }

 useEffect(
   () => {
     alert('Component Updated');
       return () => {
         alert('Component will be removed');
       };
   }
 );
```

```
 return(
   <div>
     <input id='inputTextbox'></input>
     <button type='button'
         onClick={UpdateText}>
         Update
     </button>
     <br/>
     <label>{outputValue}</label>
   </div>
 );
}

export default MyComponent;
```

In the preceding example, we are importing the useEffect() method from the React library and invoking this method in our component with an anonymous function as an input parameter. React will execute this function every time the component is rendered. Hence, you will see an alert every time you update the value of the label. Now, you might wonder that this solves our problem of performing subscription operations when the component is mounted or updated, but what about the cleanup or unsubscribe operations that we need to perform when a component is about to be unmounted?

You might think that there might be a separate method or hook to do the cleanup operations, but subscribing and unsubscribing are so closely related that React keeps them together. Cleanup operations are performed in a function returned by the anonymous function that we have passed as an input parameter to the useEffect() method. Technically, you should see an alert "Component will be removed" just before the component is about to be unmounted from the DOM. If you want to test this, write the following code in your index.js file:

```
import React from 'react';
import ReactDOM from 'react-dom';
import MyComponent from './MyComponent';

ReactDOM.render(
  <MyComponent/>,
  document.getElementById('root')
);
```

```
ReactDOM.unmountComponentAtNode(
  document.getElementById('root')
);
```

On executing this code, you will notice that you see two alert boxes, one after the other. The first one indicates that the component has been mounted, and the second one tells you that the component is about to be unmounted.

Hence, to summarize, you pass an anonymous function to the useEffect() method. Anything you write in this function body will be executed when a component is rendered. Anything that is returned by this function will be executed when the component is about to be unmounted from the DOM tree.

Custom Hooks

Custom hooks in React are normal JavaScript functions whose names are prefixed with the word "use". These functions or Hooks can be used to share stateful logic across components. Now let us consider a scenario where we want to display an alert box every time something changes in the view. We might want to do this in several components, but it is not a good practice to repeat this logic in each component we write. Hence, we can write this logic in a custom hook and share it across components. Let us understand it with the help of an example. Let us first review the code that displays an alert using the useEffect() Hook when a component is rendered:

```
import React, {useState, useEffect} from 'react';

function MyComponent(props){

 const [outputValue, setOutputValue] =
 useState('Placeholder');

 function UpdateText(){
   setOutputValue(
     document.getElementById('inputTextbox').value
   );
 }
```

```
useEffect(
  () => {
    alert('Component Updated');
    }
);

return(
  <div>
    <input id='inputTextbox'></input>
    <button type='button'
        onClick={UpdateText}>
        Update
    </button>
    <br/>
    <label>{outputValue}</label>
  </div>
 );
}

export default MyComponent;
```

What we are doing here is that we are invoking the useEffect() Hook that displays an alert whenever a component is updated. We know that a Hook can call another Hook. So, we will now create a custom Hook that will take an input argument and will display the alert for us whenever the calling component is updated. I have created a new folder "Hooks" under the "src" folder that will contain all my custom Hooks. You can follow the structure of your choice. Let us create a new file "useChangeAlert.js" for our Hook. It will contain the following code:

useChangeAlert.js

```
import {useEffect} from 'react';

export const useChangeAlert = (text) => {
  useEffect(
    () => {
      alert(text);
      }
  );
}
```

We have created a simple JavaScript function that will display an alert with the input parameter as a message whenever the calling component is updated. This will act as our custom Hook. Note that we have used React's built-in useEffect() hook to know when the calling component is re-rendered. Let us now consume this custom Hook in our component. Look at the following piece of code that goes in your MyComponent.js file:

MyComponent.js

```
import React, {useState} from 'react';
import {useChangeAlert} from './Hooks/useChangeAlert'

function MyComponent(props){

 const [outputValue, setOutputValue] =
 useState('Placeholder');

 function UpdateText(){
   setOutputValue(
     document.getElementById('inputTextbox').value
   );
 }

 useChangeAlert(`New Label Value: ${outputValue}`);

 return(
   <div>
     <input id='inputTextbox'></input>
     <button type='button'
         onClick={UpdateText}>
         Update
     </button>
     <br/>
     <label>{outputValue}</label>
   </div>
 );
}

export default MyComponent;
```

We have imported the useChangeAlert() Hook from our Hooks folder, and instead of directly invoking the useEffect() hook, we have invoked the custom Hook with the new label value as an input parameter. Also note that since we are not using the useEffect() hook in our component, we do not need to import it from the React library. If you run the code, you will notice that whenever you change the value in the input box and click the button, the label is updated and an alert is displayed with the new label value. This is done by our custom hook. You can use this custom Hook in multiple components. Let us create another component to demonstrate this. I have created an exactly similar component to our existing component. I've just changed some IDs and input that we pass to our custom Hook. Please feel free to create a component of your choice. Look at the following code for the new component that will go in a new file "MyComponent2.js":

```
import React, {useState} from 'react';
import {useChangeAlert} from './Hooks/useChangeAlert'

function MyComponent2(props){

 const [outputValue, setOutputValue] =
 useState('Placeholder');

 function UpdateText(){
   setOutputValue(
     document.getElementById('inputTextbox2').value
   );
 }

 useChangeAlert(`New Label2 Value: ${outputValue}`);

return(
   <div>
     <input id='inputTextbox2'></input>
     <button type='button'
         onClick={UpdateText}>
         Update
     </button>
     <br/>
```

```
    <label>{outputValue}</label>
  </div>
 );
}
```

```
export default MyComponent2;
```

We have imported the custom Hook and used it in a similar manner as our previous component. On click of the update button, the label should be updated and an alert box should be displayed with the new label value, just like it did for our previous component. Now the next step is to render both our components together on the same page and see how our custom hook reacts to the update operation. Consider the following piece of code that will go into our index.JS file:

```
import React from 'react';
import ReactDOM from 'react-dom';
import MyComponent from './MyComponent';
import MyComponent2 from './MyComponent2';

ReactDOM.render(
  <React.Fragment>
    <MyComponent/>
    <MyComponent2/>
  </React.Fragment>,
  document.getElementById('root')
);
```

Note that we use <React.Fragment> whenever we want to render an array of elements to the DOM. If you execute the code, you will see a browser output similar to Figure 2-5.

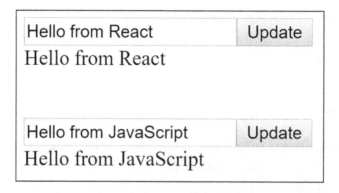

Figure 2-5. *Custom Hooks in React*

On updating either of the values and clicking their respective buttons, you will see an alert box with their respective alert messages along with the new label values. This is how stateful logic is shared across React components using custom Hooks. Let us now learn how to work with data in React components.

Working with Data

So far, we have only worked with static data. However, getting data from a remote server is very common in web applications these days. We will learn how to get data from remote APIs using asynchronous JavaScript requests in the next topic. For now, let us define a static JSON object in our application and display the data on the browser. Consider the following example:

```
import React from 'react';

const data = [
    {
        web_page: "http://www.davietjal.org/",
        state_province: "Punjab",
        name: "DAV Institute of Technology",
        country: "India"
    },
    {
        web_page: "http://www.lpu.in/",
        state_province: "Punjab",
```

```
        name: "Lovely Professional University",
        country: "India"
    },
    {

        web_page: "http://www.ddu.ac.in/",
        state_province: "Gujarat",
        name: "Dharamsinh Desai University",
        country: "India"
    }];

function MyComponent(props) {
  return (
    <div>
      <h1>Universities in India</h1>
      <br />
      {
        data.map(
          (item, index) => (
            <div key={index}>
              <h2>{item.name}</h2>
              <p>{item.state_province},
                  {item.country} </p>
              <a href={item.web_page}>Website</a>
            </div>
          )
        )
      }
    </div>
  );
}

export default MyComponent;
```

On rendering the preceding component, you should see a browser output similar to Figure 2-6.

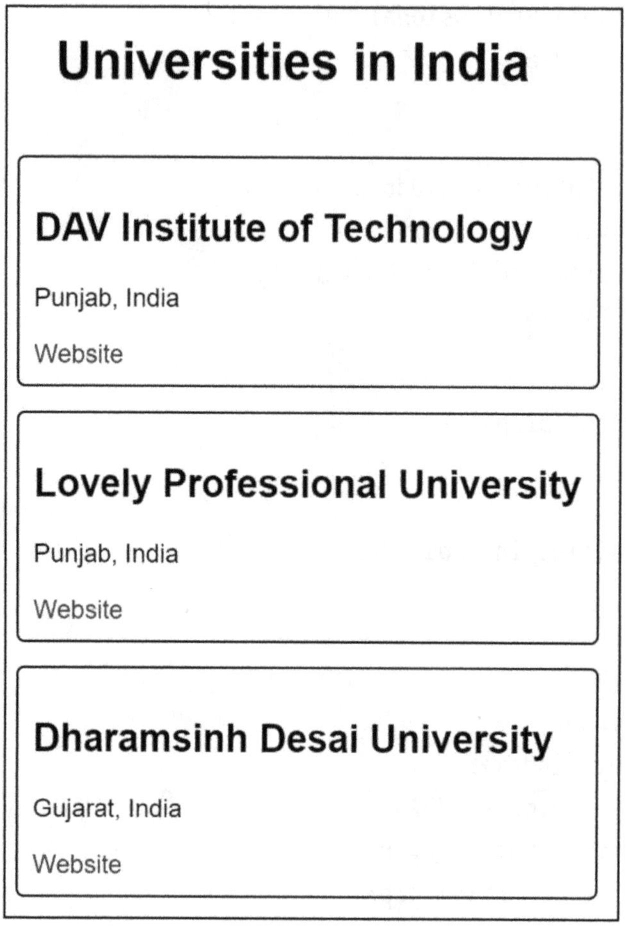

Figure 2-6. *Working with Data in React*

I have applied some basic CSS to the elements so do not worry if your output is not exactly similar to mine. You can customize your styling using your own CSS. We are using a combination of JSX and JavaScript in this component. We use JavaScript's array.map() function to iterate on our data array and execute the JSX code for each element in the data array. This is how we work with data in React components. Now, let us learn about fetching data from a remote server using asynchronous JavaScript calls.

AJAX Calls

React provides us with an option of using any of the multiple AJAX libraries which include Axios, jQuery AJAX, and the browser built-in window.fetch. In our example, we will use the Axios library to work with AJAX requests. To do so, we will need to install the library to our project using the following command:

```
$ npm install axios
```

Once Axios is installed to our project, we can import it in our component file and use its get() method to initiate a network request. We will use GitHub's public API to get a list of GitHub users and display them in our application. Consider the following example:

```
import React from 'react';
import axios from 'axios';

class MyComponent extends React.Component {

  constructor(props) {
    super(props);
    this.state = {
      error: null,
      isLoaded: false,
      data: []
    };
  }

  componentDidMount() {
    axios.get('https://api.github.com/users')
      .then(response => {
        // success
        this.setState({ data: response.data });
        this.setState({ isLoaded: true });
      })

      .catch(error => {
        // error
```

```
            this.setState({ error: error });
      })
  }

  render() {
    if (this.state.error) {
      return <div>
                Error: {this.state.error.message}
             </div>;
    }
    else if (!this.state.isLoaded) {
      return <div>Loading...</div>;
    }
    else {
      return (
        <div>
          <h1>Github Users</h1>
          <br />
          {this.state.data.map((item, index) => (
             <div key={index} className='UserBlock'>
               <img src={item.avatar_url}
                    alt='User Icon'>
               </img>

               <div className='UserDetails'>
                 <p>Username: {item.login}</p>
                 <p>ID: {item.id}</p>
               </div>
             </div>
          ))}
        </div>
      );
    }
    }
}

export default MyComponent;
```

Note that we have created a class component since we will be using componentDidMount() method to perform data operations. We have added three members to the state object in the constructor:

- **data** – This is an object that will store the data that we fetch from remote API. Initially set to an empty object.

- **error** – This is an object that will store the details of any error that occurs during the data operation. Initially set to null.

- **isLoaded** – This is a Boolean property that will tell us whether the data has been loaded into the data object or not. Initially set to false.

We use the React lifecycle method componentDidMount() to write our data fetch logic. We have used the get() method provided by Axios to make a network request to the GitHub API. Note that it is necessary to import the Axios library to our component file in order to use it. You can also use post() method provided by Axios to initiate a POST request.

Loading...

Figure 2-7. *AJAX Request in Progress*

then() method is an extension to the get() method and will be executed if the promise is fulfilled by the get() method. Hence, in this method, we have written the code that we want to execute if the network request is successful. We have filled the data object with the data that is returned by the get request and set the isLoaded property to true.

catch() method will catch any errors that occurred during the execution of the network request. In this method, we have filled the error object with the details of the error.

Error: Network Error

Figure 2-8. *Error During AJAX Request*

Then comes the render() method. Before rendering the data, we might want to check if the data has been correctly loaded or not. We also might want to check if any error has occurred during the network operation. Thus, if an error has occurred, we will simply display the error message on the browser. If the data is still loading, we will display a simple loading message on the browser. Finally, if the data has been loaded into the data object, we will iterate on the data using JavaScript's array.map() method and display the details of GitHub users on the browser. Figures 2-7, 2-8, and 2-9 show the scenarios of *Request in Progress*, *Error*, and *Success*, respectively.

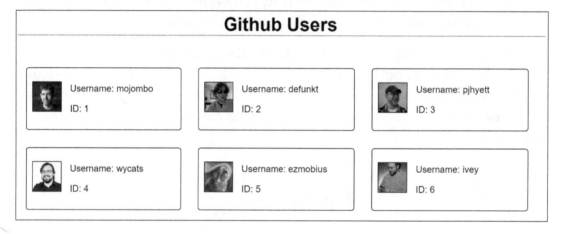

Figure 2-9. *Successful AJAX Request*

That's it, you have successfully created a data-oriented React application. You can play around with other APIs available in the public domain. For instance, you can take input from the user and fetch details for a specific GitHub user by passing username as a parameter to the API call. The more you play around, the better you will understand it.

Let us now look at how to add styling to our React application.

Styling React Components

If you have executed the previous GitHub Users application code, you must have noticed that your output slightly differs from Figure 2-9. That is because I have added some CSS to my application code in order to add styling to the elements, which might be missing from your code.

There are various ways to style your React components. Some of them are discussed in the following section.

CSS in React

Cascading Style Sheets or CSS, as we call it, is something that we have all been using every now and then in our applications. One way to use it is to simply add the style attribute in line with your JSX code as follows:

```
<div style={{ display: 'inline-block',
          marginLeft: '15px'}} >
</div>
```

There is one thing you need to take care of while using inline CSS. All the "-" encountered in CSS element keys must be replaced with camelCase format. So, instead of "margin-left", you must write "marginLeft". Note that you need not use camelCase in the values of the CSS elements. This restriction is just for the keys. So, the value "inline-block" for the key "display" will remain as it is even though it contains "-". Also, notice that we have used double curly braces to specify the value for the style attribute. This is because it accepts a JavaScript object which is defined inside the braces. You could also rewrite it as follows:

```
const divStyle = { display: 'inline-block', marginLeft: '15px'}

<div style={divStyle}>
</div>
```

Inline CSS is the least preferred way of styling your React components because it makes the code structure very messy and unreadable. A better way of using CSS is to create a separate stylesheet and import it in your component file or root application file. That is the approach I have followed for our previous example. The following is the stylesheet I have written for the GitHub Users example:

Index.css

```
body{
  font-family: sans-serif;
}

#root div h1{
    text-align: center;
}
```

```
img{
  height:50px;
  width:50px;
  border: 1px solid black;
}

.UserBlock{
  display: inline-block;
  border: 1px solid black;
  border-radius: 5px;
  padding: 10px;
  margin: 15px;
  width:255px;
}

.UserDetails{
  display: inline-block;
  margin-left:15px;
}
```

I have imported this stylesheet in the root JavaScript file "index.js" using the following line of code:

```
...
import './index.css'
...
```

In your component file "MyComponent.js", you can specify the name of the CSS class for the element in JSX code using the "className" attribute as follows:

```
<div className='UserBlock'>
</div>
```

This is a much better approach as compared to inline CSS and results in a much better code structure as well as lesser code size due to the reusability of the stylesheet.

SASS and SCSS in React

SASS is the most popular option when it comes to styling React applications. It stands for Syntactically Awesome Style Sheets and is a preprocessor that compiles the input into CSS code. The newer version of SASS is known by the name SCSS (Sassy CSS) and has a slightly different syntax as compared to SASS. Both SASS and SCSS are similar to CSS stylesheets but are much powerful with support for CSS variables and mathematical operations.

SASS has a loose syntax that uses indentation instead of curly braces to indicate nesting of selectors and newlines instead of semicolons to separate properties. These stylesheets have ".sass" file extension.

SCSS, on the other hand, is closer to CSS syntax with the use of curly brackets to indicate nesting of selectors and semicolons for separation of properties. This is why every CSS stylesheet is a valid SCSS stylesheet with identical interpretation. These stylesheets have ".scss" file extension. Consider the following example that demonstrates SASS and SCSS:

Index.sass

```
$br: 5px

.UserBlock
    border-radius: $br
```

Index.scss

```
$br: 5px;

.UserBlock{
    border-radius: $br;
}
```

You can define variables using the "$" symbol and use it throughout the stylesheet. Another interesting concept provided by SCSS is Mixin. A Mixin allows us to create a block of CSS code that we might reuse throughout our stylesheet. Consider the following example:

```
@mixin black-border {
  border: 1px solid black;
}
```

```
div {
  @include black-border;
}

p {
  @include black-border;
}
```

Two important keywords to note here are "@mixin" and "@include". In SASS, these keywords are replaced by "=" and "+". We create a Mixin using the former keyword and use it throughout our stylesheet with the help of the latter. The SASS equivalent of the preceding SCSS code is as follows:

```
=black-border
  border: 1px solid black

div
  +black-border

p
  +black-border
```

You can also pass a parameter to a Mixin as follows:

Style.scss

```
@mixin custom-border($color) {
  border: 1px solid $color;
}

div {
  @include custom-border(black);
}

p {
  @include custom-border(blue);
}
```

Style.sass

```
=custom-border($color)
  border: 1px solid $color
```

```
div
    +custom-border(black)

p
    +custom-border(blue)
```

SASS and SCSS have a dependency on a module called "sass-loader". This module is dependent on "react-scripts". If you have created your React application using the "create-react-app" command, then "react-scripts" is already added to the JSON file as a dependency and all the dependencies of "react-scripts" including "sass-loader" are installed in the node_modules folder. However, there is still one module that you will have to install. That is "node-sass". It is responsible for compiling SASS or SCSS to CSS. You can install it using the following command:

```
npm install node-sass
```

Once this is installed in your project, you can start using SASS and SCSS without any further configuration. All you need in this case is a ".sass" or ".scss" file and you are good to go.

However, if you have not used the "create-react-app" command to create your React applications, you will need to manually install the dependencies using the following command:

```
npm install react-scripts
npm install node-sass
```

There are many other ways to add styling to your application such as Styled Components, Less, CSS Modules, and so on. However, in my opinion, SASS and SCSS are better than the other approaches.

That's it about styling. Let us now look at Babel and Webpack.

Babel and Webpack

Babel is a JavaScript compiler that has solved a very big problem for the entire community of developers – backward compatibility. We all have faced issues with browsers like Internet Explorer and Edge not being able to support the latest JavaScript functionalities. For instance, arrow functions introduced in ES6 are supported by most of the modern browsers but not by IE 11. In such cases, Babel comes to the rescue. It takes code written in one standard, and it compiles it to code written in another standard. However, Babel is not going to compile anything by itself. We will have to install several plugins to support a particular feature in older browsers.

Webpack, on the other hand, is a module bundler that handles bundling and minification of our application files. It goes through our application and creates a list of all the modules that our application is dependent on in order to function correctly. Then it creates a pluggable bundle or package which contains the minimum number of files required for our application. It generally requires a webpack.config.js file where we specify the entry point for our application and other relevant information regarding the application output.

Babel can easily be installed using the following npm command:

```
npm install @babel/core @babel/cli babel-loader
```

@babel/core is the module that allows us to run babel. @babel/cli is used to run babel from the terminal. babel-loader is the module that allows us to teach webpack how to identify and run files related to babel. As discussed earlier, to make babel translate our code to a backward-compatible version, we will have to add certain plugins for babel. Let's try installing the plugin that converts arrow functions to regular JavaScript functions. Use the following command to do so:

```
npm install @babel/plugin-transform-arrow-functions
```

Now, in order to configure babel, we will need to create a .babelrc file in the root directory of our application and add the following code to it:

```
{
  "plugins": ["@babel/transform-arrow-functions "]
}
```

Now let's create the following script.js file to test whether babel is working correctly or not:

Script.js

```
var a = () => {};
var b = (c) => c;
```

If you run "npx babel src\Script.js" command in the terminal, you will see the following output:

```
var a = function () {};
var b = function (c) {
  return c;
};
```

As you can see, babel successfully converts arrow functions to normal JavaScript functions in order to make them compatible with older browsers. There are many other plugins that you can install and use in your application. However, in a big application, you might require a large number of plugins, and installing them one by one is not practical. To solve this problem, we have something called babel presets that groups certain plugins required for a particular kind of application. You can directly install a babel preset rather than installing multiple plugins one by one. The following are the two babel presets important while creating a React application:

- **@babel/preset-env** – Converts ES6, ES7, and ES8 code to ES5

- **@babel/preset-react** – Transforms JSX to JavaScript

Let us install these two presets using the following code:

```
npm install @babel/preset-env
npm install @babel/preset-react
```

Now that we have installed these presets, we will also need to add it to the .babelrc file. Refer to the following code for the same:

```
{
    "presets": [
        "@babel/preset-env",
        "@babel/preset-react"
    ]
}
```

Let us now add the following JSX code to our Script.js file and see how babel compiles it:

```
ReactDOM.render(<MyComponent/>,
                document.getElementById('root'));
```

If you run the "npx babel src\Script.js" command once again in the terminal, you will see the following output:

```
ReactDOM.render(
  React.createElement(MyComponent, null),
  document.getElementById('root')
);
```

As you can see, babel converts the JSX code to equivalent JavaScript code so that older browsers can understand it. So far, we have been testing babel through the terminal. Let us see how to add it to our application bundle with the help of webpack. Use the following command to install webpack to your application:

```
npm install webpack webpack-cli
```

Once installed, webpack needs a config file "webpack.config.js" in the root directory of your application. Let us create that file and add the following code to it:

```
const path = require('path');

module.exports = {
  entry: './src/app.js',
  output: {
    path: path.join(__dirname, 'public'),
    filename: 'bundle.js'
  }
};
```

Now, it is time for webpack to learn how to use babel on runtime in order to compile JSX code into JavaScript code. To do so, we will have to add some code to the config file. Refer to the following updated config file for the webpack:

```
const path = require('path');

module.exports = {
  entry: './src/app.js',
  output: {
    path: path.join(__dirname, 'public'),
    filename: 'bundle.js'
  },
```

```
module: {
  rules: [
    {
      test: /\.js$/,
      exclude: /node_modules/,
      loader: 'babel-loader'
    }
  ]
}
};
```

A loader lets us customize the behavior of the webpack when it loads certain files. We can define a loader by setting the module property to an array of rules in the webpack. config file. In this case, we have set the "loader" property of the rule to babel-loader which will tell the webpack to convert the JSX code to JavaScript code. The "test" property allows us to specify what kind of files we want to run the loader on. We specify a pattern for files that end with ".js". We can use the "exclude" property to exclude a set of files. In our case, we exclude the node_modules folder since we do not want babel to scan those files.

Note   The code snippets that you have seen in this topic are not enough to create a full-fledged React application. There are lots of other webpack configurations that you need to do. However, if you have created your application using the "create-react-app" command, everything is pre-configured and you need not worry about configuring webpack.

That is it. Webpack is now set to identify JSX code and compile it to JavaScript code using babel. With that, we come to the end of this chapter. Let us summarize what we have learned.

Summary

- React.js is an open source JavaScript library that is used for building user interfaces.

- React generates HTML using JavaScript. It renders everything in form of Component.

- Components in React are similar to JavaScript functions. They take in input parameters and output UI elements. Components can be used like HTML elements.

- When the state of a component changes, the UI changes automatically.

- Changes in UI are compared using virtual DOM since the actual DOM is not accessible until UI is rendered.

- Single-page applications, Immutability, purity, and composition are some of the important concepts related to React.

- "create-react-app" command can be used to create a starter application in React. To do so, you will need Node.js environment and Node Package Manager (npm) installed in your system.

- You can either create React components using traditional JavaScript syntax or use the modern JSX syntax which is much closer to HTML.

- There are two approaches to create a React component – classes and functions.

- The class component allows you to extend React.Component class and inherit React lifecycle methods as well as the state object. To do so in function components, you need Hooks.

- You can use the State Hook to create a stateful function component, whereas to step into lifecycle methods of React in a function component, you can use Effect Hook. You can also create custom Hooks that suit your application requirements.

- The lifecycle of a React component includes mounting, updating, and unmounting.

- render() method gets invoked every time a component is updated or when it mounted for the first time.

- componentDidMount() method tells us that the component has been mounted, and componentDidUpdate() method tells us that the component has been updated.

- componentWillUnmount() method gets invoked just before a component is about to be unmounted from the DOM.

- You can fetch data for your application from a remote resource using the Axios library for AJAX calls. You can use JavaScript's array.map() function to iterate on an array data.

- componentDidMount() is the ideal place to initiate network requests for getting data.

- SASS and SCSS are the most popular alternatives to style your React application.

- Babel is a JavaScript compiler that is used to add backward compatibility to your code.

- Webpack is a module bundler that handles bundling and minification of your application files.

CHAPTER 3

Next.js

In the previous chapter, we learned about a JavaScript framework called React.js and how to create a client-side rendered application using the React.js framework. In this chapter, we will learn about a framework called "Next.js" that is used to build applications that are rendered on the server-side.

We will learn about the features of Next.js framework, routing in an application built using Next.js, dynamically loading the content, and configuring webpack and Babel, among other things. We will also create an interactive Next.js application from scratch as a part of this chapter.

Subsequently, we will learn how to integrate frameworks such as Redux for state management and GraphQL for API queries to our Next.js application. Let us get started.

Introduction to Next.js

Next.js is a framework that helps us render applications on the server-side. As discussed in the previous chapter, when you create a React application, all the content is rendered to the browser using client-side JavaScript. There are several problems associated with this. The following is a brief list:

- Clients who do not have JavaScript enabled in their browsers might not be able to view the content.

- We might simply want to render certain content on the server-side due to security reasons, which is not possible in a plain React.js application.

- Rendering everything on the client-side significantly increases the loading time of the application.

- It is difficult for search engines to index single-page applications built using plain React.js.

© Mohit Thakkar 2020
M. Thakkar, *Building React Apps with Server-Side Rendering*, https://doi.org/10.1007/978-1-4842-5869-9_3

All these problems can be solved with the help of server-side rendering. Next.js is a framework that provides us just that. Every time a request is received, it dynamically generates a page at runtime with the help of a server. It is used by leading companies such as Netflix, Docker, GitHub, Uber, Starbucks, and many more. Let us look at the features of the Next.js framework.

Features of Next.js

The following are some of the major features of Next.js framework:

- **Hot reloading** – Every time a change is detected on a page, Next.js reloads the page so that the change is immediately reflected.

- **Page-based routing** – URLs are mapped to the "pages" folder on the file system for you to use it without any configuration. However, dynamic routes are supported as well.

- **Automatic code splitting** – Pages are loaded with just the code that they need which results in faster loading.

- **Page prefetching** – You can use the "prefetch" prop on the <Link> tag while linking pages in order to prefetch pages in the background.

- **Hot module replacement (HMR)** – You can replace, add, or remove modules from an application on runtime using HMR.

- **Server-side rendering (SSR)** – You can render the page from the server-side instead of generating the entire HTML on the client-side. This results in a shorter loading time for content-rich pages. SSR also ensures that your pages are easily indexable by search engines.

Let us look at these features in action by getting started with our own Next.js application.

Getting Started

In order to get started with your own Next.js application, it is necessary that you have Node.js installed on your system. You must have installed it while practicing React.js examples during the previous chapter. If you have not, you can download and install it from `https://nodejs.org/`. Once it is installed, you can open a terminal in your editor and run "node -v" command to check if the node.js has installed correctly. If yes, the terminal will display the installed version number of Node.js. We will be using npm (Node Package Manager) to initialize our application and install dependencies to our project. npm comes bundled along with Node.js and should already be installed in your system if you have installed Node.js. You can execute "npm -v" command in the terminal. If installed correctly, this command will display the version of npm installed in your system.

I'll be using the Visual Studio Code editor which can be downloaded from `https://code.visualstudio.com/download`. However, you can use any editor of your choice.

Once you are done with the installation, you can create a directory for your Next.js application. I have created a directory with the name "my-next-app". We will now navigate to this newly created directory from the terminal and run the "npm init" command to create a package.json file. While running this command, you might have to enter some values such as package name, version, description, git repository, keywords, and so on for the JSON file. You can choose to go forward with the default values or enter some values of your own. On successful execution of the "npm init" command, you might notice that a package.json file is created in the directory. It should have the following code:

```
{
  "name": "my-next-app",
  "version": "1.0.0",
  "description": "My Next.js Application",
  "main": "index.js",
  "scripts": {
    "test": "echo \"Error: no test specified\" &&
            exit 1"
  },
  "author": "Mohit Thakkar",
  "license": "ISC"
}
```

The values might differ if you have specified a different set of values during initialization. We will now install next, react, and react-dom to our application using the following command:

```
npm install react react-dom next --save
```

The "--save" command will instruct npm to add the installed packages to the package.json file as dependencies. If you check the file, you will have the following section added to it:

```
"dependencies": {
  "next": "^9.1.5",
  "react": "^16.12.0",
  "react-dom": "^16.12.0"
}
```

In order to start a server, we will have to specify the start script in the package.json file. Let's add that by replacing the scripts section in the file with the following code:

```
"scripts": {
  "start": "next"
}
```

Now that you have specified the start script, you might want to launch the server and start your application. You can do that using the "npm start" command. However, at this point in time, you won't be able to do so because a Next.js application looks for a startup page in the "pages" folder at the application launch. Since we do not have a "pages" folder yet, we will get a compile-time error when we try to launch our application. Let us create an empty "pages" folder at the root of our application. Once created, you can launch your application using the "npm start" command. You will notice a 404 error when you navigate to the application URL – http://localhost:3000/ – on the server. This is shown in Figure 3-1.

Figure 3-1. *Next.js Application Startup*

Notice the sleek and user-friendly design of this error page. This is how Next. js handles errors. It can also handle other errors such as 500 – Internal Server Error. The cause of the 404 error is that there are no pages in our application. On application launch, Next.js tries to find the "index.js" file in the pages and renders it by default. In our case, since it is not able to find it, we are greeted with a 404 error. Let us now create our first page. Add "index.js" file to the "pages" folder with the following code:

Pages/index.js

```
import React from "react";

function MyComponent(){
    return(
        <div>Hello from Next.js!</div>
    );
}

export default MyComponent;
```

Now, if you launch the server using the "npm start" command and browse to http://localhost:3000/ or http://localhost:3000/Index, you will be able to see the page that you just created, as shown in Figure 3-2.

Hello from Next.js!

Figure 3-2. *First Page in Next.js*

Let us now test if the content is really getting rendered on the server-side. If you right-click the page and view the page source, you will notice that the HTML content generated in code is directly getting filled into the root HTML tags. This is because everything is being rendered on the server-side. If you do the same for an application built using plain React.js, you will notice just the root HTML tags in the page source and not the content generated by the code. This is because, in a React.js application, the content is rendered on the client-side after the page gets loaded. Thus, we can be assured the Next.js renders our pages on the server-side.

In the next section, we will create another page for our application and see how to navigate between pages using Next.js routing.

Routing in Next.js

So far, we have had only one page, but an application might have multiple pages and easy navigation between those pages is an important aspect of any application. Let us create an "About" page with the following code:

Pages/about.js

```
import React from "react";

function About(){
    return(
        <div>
            This is an application built using next.js to demonstrate the
            effectiveness of server-side rendering!
        </div>
    );
}

export default About;
```

If you run the application and navigate to `http://localhost:3000/About`, you shall see the page you just created, similar to Figure 3-3. Not that you do not have to restart the npm process in order to see the changes. As soon as you save any changes, Next. js performs hot reloading and you can see the changes without restarting the server. However, you might have to refresh the browser page.

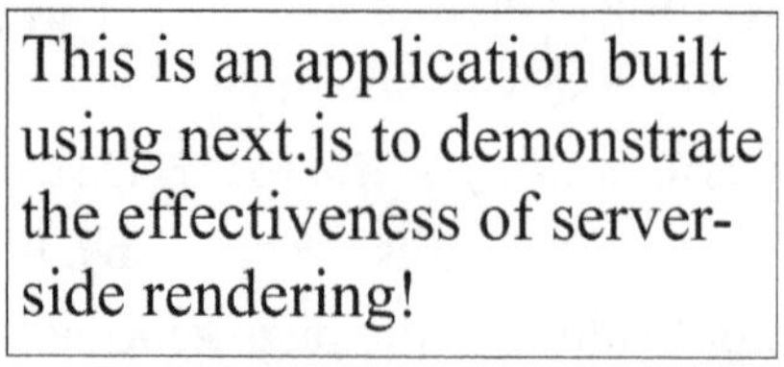

This is an application built using next.js to demonstrate the effectiveness of server-side rendering!

Figure 3-3. *Second Page in Next.js*

Now, to establish a link between the two pages, you might think of creating an anchor tag with the page URL passed to the "href" attribute. Let us do that and see what's happening:

Pages/index.js

```
import React from "react";

function MyComponent(){
    return(
        <div>
            <p>Hello from Next.js!</p>
            <a href='/About'>About</a>
        </div>
    );
}

export default MyComponent;
```

If you run the app, you will see a link to the "About" page. However, if you click the link, you will notice that the entire page gets reloaded. This is because the anchor tag sends a new request to the server and the routing will happen server-side. This might result in performance issues so you might want to keep the routing to the client-side.

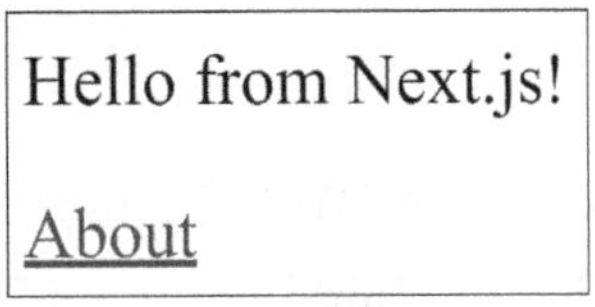

```
Hello from Next.js!

About
```

Figure 3-4. *Routing in Next.js*

Next.js provides <Link> component for creating links for client-side routing. It is a wrapper that works with any component that accepts "onClick" prop. Hence, we will use it with an empty anchor tag. Consider the following change in the code:

Pages/index.js

```
import React from "react";
import Link from 'next/link'
```

```
function MyComponent(){
    return(
        <div>
            <p>Hello from Next.js!</p>
            <Link href='/About'>
                <a>About</a>
            </Link>
        </div>
    );
}

export default MyComponent;
```

In order to use the `<Link>` component, you will have to first import it from the "next/link" module. On executing the preceding code, you will have the same output as Figure 3-4, but when you click the link, you will notice that no additional server request is generated on the network. You can verify this in the "Network" tab in the Chrome browser's developer tools window. This is because the client-side routing is at work here. Page specified in the <Link> component will be prefetched, and the navigation will happen without a server request.

Most scenarios of client-side routing break the browser navigation buttons. However, Next.js has full support for the History API so it won't break your browser navigation buttons.

Note   The History API lets you interact with the browser history, trigger the browser navigation methods, and change the address bar content. It is especially useful in single-page applications where you never really change the page, just the content is changed. A stack is maintained. Every time the user navigates within the same web site, the URL of the new page is placed at the top of the stack. Whenever the user triggers the browser navigation buttons, the pointer of the stack is adjusted and the appropriate content is rendered.

That is it about routing in Next.js. Let us now look at dynamic pages in Next.js.

Dynamic Pages

Most of the real-time applications have content that is generated dynamically. Hence, we cannot rely on static pages in a practical scenario. Let's see how to generate dynamic content for our application. First of all, we will create a file, DynamicRouter.js, that will create links based on the props. Consider the following code:

SharedComponents/DynamicRouter.js

```
import React from "react";
import Link from 'next/link'

function GetLink(props) {
    return (
        <div>
            <Link href="">
                <a>{props.title}</a>
            </Link>
        </div>
    );
}

export default GetLink;
```

Pages/index.js

```
import React from "react";
import GetLink from "../SharedComponents/DynamicRouter";

function MyComponent(){
    return(
        <div>
            <GetLink title='Page 1'></GetLink>
            <GetLink title='Page 2'></GetLink>
            <GetLink title='Page 3'></GetLink>
        </div>
    );
}

export default MyComponent;
```

If you see the browser window, you will notice three links generated on the index page, as shown in Figure 3-5. However, these are empty links and will not navigate to any page.

Figure 3-5. *Dynamic Links in Next.js*

Let us now create a page that will dynamically display content based on the parameter it receives. We will then set these three links to navigate to this dynamic page with different parameters. Consider the following code for the new page:

Pages/SecondPage.js

```
export default (props) => (
    <h1>
        Welcome to {props.url.query.content}
    </h1>
);
```

SharedComponents/DynamicRouter.js

```
...
<Link href={`/SecondPage?content=${props.title}`}>
    <a>{props.title}</a>
</Link>
...
```

Now if you click the links, you will be redirected to a page that loads the content dynamically, as shown in Figure 3-6.

Figure 3-6. *Dynamic Page in Next.js*

If you notice the URL that gets generated, you will see that the query parameters are displayed on the address bar. You might want users to see a clean URL that does not display the query parameters. This is possible in Next.js by using the "as" attribute of the "Link" component. Whatever you pass to the "as" attribute will be displayed in the address bar. Let us try this:

Pages/index.js

```
...
    <GetLink title='Page 1' Disp='page-1'>
    </GetLink>
    <GetLink title='Page 2' Disp='page-2'>
    </GetLink>
    <GetLink title='Page 3' Disp='page-3'>
    </GetLink>
...
```

SharedComponents/DynamicRouter.js

```
...
<Link href={`/SecondPage?content=${props.title}`}
    as={props.Disp}>
    <a>{props.title}</a>
</Link>
...
```

Now, if you click the links and navigate to one of the pages, you will see a clean URL without any parameters, as in Figure 3-7.

Figure 3-7. *Custom URL for a Next.js Page*

That is it about dynamic pages in Next.js. Let us now learn how to deal with multimedia content in a Next.js application.

Adding Multimedia Content Using CSS

At times you might want to add multimedia content such as images and videos to your application. Generally, it is preferred to add URLs to such content in the CSS itself so that it is easy to maintain. Let us add images next to the links on the index page. I have downloaded three images and added them to the "static/Images" folder at the root of our application. Next.js provides something called JSS (CSS in JS) which allows us to define styles directly inside JSX code. Let us add the following code to "index.js" file to add images using CSS:

index.js

```
...
return (
 <div>
  ...
  <style jsx global>
  {`
    a{
      color:blue;
    }
```

```
    .img{
        height: 50px;
        width: 50px;
        background-size: cover!important;
        background-repeat: no-repeat!important;
        background-position: center!important;
        border: 1px solid black;
        border-radius: 10px;
        display: inline-block;
        margin-top: 10px;
    }
    .p1{
        background: url(../static/Images/1.jpg);
    }

    .p2{
        background: url(../static/Images/2.jpg);
    }

    .p3{
        background: url(../static/Images/3.jpg);
    }
  `}
  </style>
 </div>
);
...
```

Now that we have defined the styles, we might want to use these styles on our page. To do so, we need to pass the class name from "index.js" file as a prop to the `<Link>` component and use it in "DynamicRouter.js" file to create a `<div>` for the image and set the class name for it. Consider the following changes to code:

Index.js

```
...
  <GetLink title='Page 1'
          Disp='page-1'
          Class='img p1'>
  </GetLink>
  <GetLink title='Page 2'
          Disp='page-2'
          Class='img p2'>
  </GetLink>
  <GetLink title='Page 3'
          Disp='page-3'
          Class='img p3'>
  </GetLink>
...
```

DynamicRouter.js

```
...
return (
        <div>
            <div className={props.Class}></div>
            <Link
      href={`/SecondPage?content=${props.title}`}
      as={props.Disp}>
                    <a>{props.title}</a>
            </Link>
        </div>
);
...
```

If you save the changes, you will see a browser output similar to Figure 3-8.

Figure 3-8. *Multimedia Content in Next.js*

You might want to create a separate CSS file for all your styles. However, you cannot directly do that in a Next.js application. You will have to first install a CSS loader. You can install @zeit/next-css module to your application using the following command:

```
npm install @zeit/next-css --save
```

Once installed, you will have to add a config file "next.config.js" to the root of your application with the following code:

Next.config.js

```
const withCSS = require('@zeit/next-css')
module.exports = withCSS({})
```

Now, you will have to create a file "style.css" in the root of your application. You can then remove the <style jsx global> component from "index.js" file and move the stylesheet code to the "style.css" file as follows:

```
a{
    color:blue;
}
```

```
.img{
    height: 50px;
    width: 50px;
    background-size: cover!important;
    background-repeat: no-repeat!important;
    background-position: center!important;
    border: 1px solid black;
    border-radius: 10px;
    display: inline-block;
    margin-top: 10px;
}

.p1{
    background: url(/static/Images/1.jpg);
}

.p2{
    background: url(/static/Images/2.jpg);
}

.p3{
    background: url(/static/Images/3.jpg);
}
```

Note that it is important that your images are placed inside the "static" folder which is at the same level in your application as the "pages" folder. In your "index.js" file, you will be able to import the CSS file like any other file using the following line of code:

```
import "../style.css";
```

If you save the changes and go to the browser window, you will see output similar to Figure 3-8. All other multimedia content including videos can be rendered to your application in a similar manner. Let us now see how to get data from a remote server in a Next.js application.

Getting Data from Remote Server

You might remember that in the previous chapter, we used the Axios library to perform AJAX requests in order to get data from a remote endpoint. We will do the same thing in our Next.js application. The difference here is that instead of the client-side, the AJAX call will be performed on the server-side. Firstly, we will install the Axios library to our project using the following command:

```
$ npm install axios
```

Once it is installed, we can use its get() method in our page to fetch the data from a remote endpoint. However, things will change a little bit in a Next.js application. Previously, we performed the AJAX call in the component's componentDidMount() method. But in this case, we will use a special method, getInitialProps(), provided by Next.js which helps us set the props for a component. We will initiate our Axios request in the getInitialProps() method. Consider the following page that uses GitHub's public API to get a list of GitHub users and display them in our application:

Pages/GithubUsers.js

```
import React from 'react'
import axios from 'axios';
import '../style.css';

export default class extends React.Component {
  static async getInitialProps() {
    try {
        const res = await axios.get('https://api.github.com/users');
        return { data: res.data }
      }catch(e){
        return {error:e}
      }
    }

    render() {
      if (this.props.error) {
        return (
```

```
            <div>
               Error: {this.props.error.message}
            </div>
         );
      }
      else {
         return (
            <div>
               <h1>Github Users</h1>
               <br />
               {this.props.data.map((item, index) => (
                  <div key={index}
className='UserBlock'>
                     <img src={item.avatar_url}
                        alt='User Icon'>
      </img>

                     <div className='UserDetails'>
                        <p>Username: {item.login}</p>
                        <p>ID: {item.id}</p>
                     </div>
                  </div>
               ))}
            </div>
         );
      }
   }
}
```

Since Axios requests are asynchronous, we need a way to catch the response when it becomes available. Previously, we did this using the then() extension method of the Axios library's get() method. This time, we have used the await keyword with the Axios method call and marked the getInitialProps() method as asynchronous. async... await keyword helps us deal with asynchronous requests without having to use callbacks or promises and is convenient for our application. We wrap this request in a try... catch block so that we can know if an error occurs on the network. Once the request is processed, we return an object from the getInitialProps() method containing either data or error. The object returned by this method will be set to the props object. In the render method, we check if the error exists by checking the error property using "this. props.error". If it does, the user will see an error message on the browser, similar to Figure 3-9.

Error: Request failed with status code 404

Figure 3-9. *Error in Axios Request*

If there is no error, then we will iterate over "this.props.data" object using JavaScript's array.map() method and display the details of GitHub users on the browser. The output should look similar to Figure 3-10.

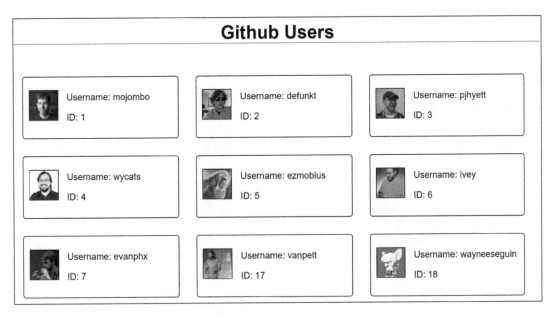

Figure 3-10. *Successful Axios Request*

If your output is a bit different than the one in Figure 3-10, do not worry. There is one thing that is still missing from your code. I have added some styles to the "style.css" file that we created earlier and imported it in our page. Do the same, and you are good to go with the styling. You can refer to the following stylesheet code:

style.css

```css
body {
    font-family: sans-serif;
}

body div h1 {
    text-align: center;
    border-bottom: 1px solid grey;
}

img {
    height: 50px;
    width: 50px;
    border: 1px solid black;
}

.UserBlock {
    display: inline-block;
    border: 1px solid black;
    border-radius: 5px;
    padding: 10px;
    margin: 15px;
    width: 255px;
}

.UserDetails {
    display: inline-block;
    margin-left: 15px;
}

.error {
    color: red;
    font-weight: bold;
    font-size: 26px;
    text-align: center;
}
```

That's it. You can now fetch data from any remote endpoint and use it in your application.

Creating Interactive App Using Next.js

Let's try to add some user interaction to our application. We will get the GitHub user id as text input from the browser and will display user details for that particular GitHub user. To do so, we will need to get the initial data from props and set it in our state object using constructor, just like we did in the previous chapter for a traditional React application. The only difference here is that the props will come from `getInitialProps()` method.

Note   We need to transfer the props to the state object because props object is not editable and, hence, we cannot directly use it for data operations.

When an id is entered from the browser, we will make an API call to fetch user details and modify the data in the state object. As soon as the state object changes, React will re-render the UI. Consider the following code:

Pages/GithubUsers.js

```
import React from 'react';
import axios from 'axios';
import '../style.css';

export default class extends React.Component {

  static async getInitialProps() {
    try {
      const res = await axios.get('https://api.github.com/users');
      return { data: res.data }
    } catch (e) {
      return { error: e }
    }
  }
```

```
constructor(props) {
  super(props);
  this.state = {data: props.data,
                error: props.error };
}

GetUser = async () =>
{
  try {
    const res = await axios.get('https://api.github.com/users/' +
    document.getElementById('inputTextbox').value);
    this.setState({
      data: [res.data],
      error: null
    });

  } catch (e) {
    this.setState({
      data: null,
      error: e
    });
  }
}

render() {
  if (this.state.error) {
    return(
      <div>
        <h1>Github Users</h1>
        <br />
        <div className='center'>
          <input id='inputTextbox' type='text'>
          </input>
          <button type='button'
                  onClick={this.GetUser}>
            Get User
          </button>
        </div>
```

```
          <br />
          <p className="error">
            Error: {this.state.error.message}</p>
        </div>
      );
  }
  else {
    return (
      <div>
        <h1>Github Users</h1>
        <br />
        <div className='center'>
          <input id='inputTextbox' type='text'>
          </input>
          <button type='button'
                  onClick={this.GetUser}>
            Get User
          </button>
        </div>
        <br />
        {this.state.data.map((item, index) => (
          <div key={index} className='UserBlock'>
            <img src={item.avatar_url}
                 alt='User Icon'></img>
            <div className='UserDetails'>
              <p>Username: {item.login}</p>
              <p>ID: {item.id}</p>
            </div>
          </div>
        ))}
      </div>
    );
  }
 }
}
```

The following is a list of things we are doing in the preceding piece of code:

- getInitialProps() method gets the initial list of Github users and returns the data that is set as props for the page. These props can be accessed using "this.props" and are not editable.

- constructor() method initializes the state object with the values passed as props. This state object will be updated every time we fetch GitHub user details for a specific user requested.

- GetUser() method handles the click event of the button and makes an API call every time the user requests details for a specific GitHub user. The user id for the GitHub is fetched from the input textbox and is sent as a parameter to the API call. The state object is updated with the data returned by the API call. As soon as the state object is updated, React re-renders the view.

- render() method checks the state object and renders the UI with user details if the request is successful or an error message if there is an error in the request.

If you navigate to the "GithubUsers" page on the browser and search for a valid user, you will see the details for that user, as shown in Figure 3-11.

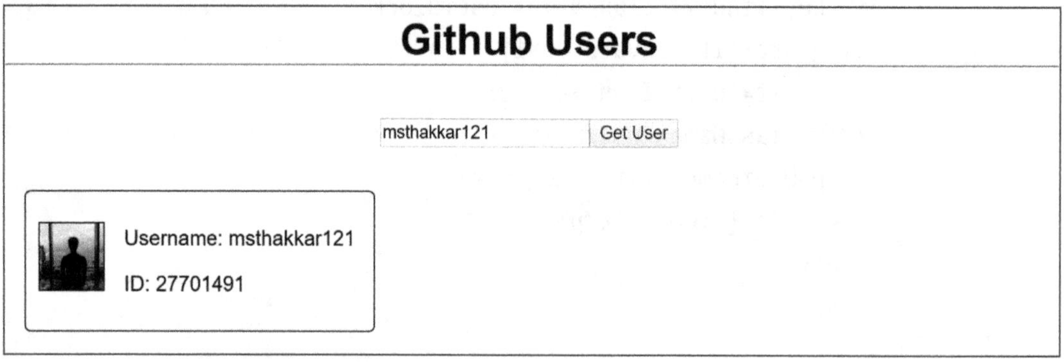

Figure 3-11. *Interactive Next.js Application*

If you search for a non-existent user, you will see an error message as shown in Figure 3-12. You can customize the error message as per your preference.

Figure 3-12. *GitHub User Not Found*

That is it. We have just created an interactive application that renders the content on the server-side using Next.js and React.js. Let us now learn how to manage the state of our application using Redux.

Using Redux with Next.js

Most of the large-scale applications in the market use MVC architecture for state management. However, implementing MVC in applications built using client-side libraries is a painful task because unlike a central model in traditional MVC, the State in a client-side application is scattered across pages and is not at the application level. To implement MVC-style state management in client-side libraries, we use Redux. The architecture of Redux is shown in Figure 3-13.

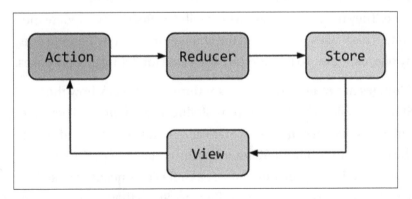

Figure 3-13. *Redux Architecture*

Here is what you need to know in order to understand Redux architecture:

- The view triggers an Action which in turn updates the Store with the help of Reducers. The Store then implicitly sends the updated data back to the View.

- Actions pass the information to the Reducer, and then based on the information received, the Reducer decides what data to update in the Store.

- A Store can be visualized as an application-level State object. Change in this object will trigger View updates.

- Actions are the special methods that update the application State whenever a change in the View triggers these methods.

- Unlike the traditional MVC pattern, the data flow here is unidirectional. This means that the Store cannot trigger any Actions. Only the View can trigger Actions. This significantly reduces the possibility of infinite loops.

You will understand it better as we start working with an example. Let us look at three fundamental principles of Redux:

1. **Single source of truth** – The state of the entire application resides in a single Store object.

2. **State is read-only** – The only way to change a State is by triggering an Action. Views do not have the privilege to directly update the State. They trigger an Action which tells the Reducer to update the State. This makes sure that all the changes to the State happen one by one, centrally, so that they are traceable for debugging purposes.

3. **Changes are made with pure functions** – To specify how the State is modified by Actions, pure Reducers are written. These are functions that take in current State and Action as input and return the next State as output. Remember the concept of purity that we studied in the previous chapter as a Basic Concept of React? That is exactly what Reducers adhere to. Since they got to be pure functions, make sure that they return a new State object instead of modifying the existing one.

Note   A pure function never modifies the values of input parameters. It rather returns a new object every time it is invoked. Also, no matter how many times you invoke a pure function, it will always return the same output for the same set of input parameters. Lastly, a pure function depends only on its input parameters and never modifies anything outside of its scope.

Let us learn about Store, Reducers, and Actions in a bit more detail.

Store

Store is the object that stores the State of the entire application. As discussed earlier, it is the "Single source of truth". A store can be easily created using the following code snippet:

```
import {createStore} from 'redux';
import reducer from 'reducer';

const store = createStore(reducer);
```

The following are some of the methods provided by the Store object:

- **store.getState()** – This method returns the current state.

- **store.dispatch(action)** – Update the State by dispatching the action. The Reducer function associated with the Store will be called with the current State and the action. Its return value will be considered as the next state. The change listeners will also be immediately notified as soon as the State changes.

- **store.subscribe(listener)** – It is used to add a change listener to the State. You can pass a function as a parameter. This function will be called every time an action is dispatched. You can use the getState() method in the listener to get the updated State value.

- **unsubscribe()** – This method is used when you no longer want to call your listener method when the State changes. This method is returned when you subscribe to a listener so you might want to save it in a variable during subscribing in order to be able to unsubscribe. Consider the following code snippet:

```
// Subscribing
const unsubscribe = store.subscribe(someListener);

// Unsubscribing
unsubscribe();
```

Actions

Actions are payloads of information that send data from your application to your store. They are plain JavaScript objects which contain a type and an optional payload. They are the only source of information for the store. The following code snippet demonstrates an Action being created and dispatched:

```
...
const action = {
  type: 'Multiply',
  payload: { value: 10 },
};
store.dispatch(action)
```

Redux does not have a strict rule set for defining your Actions. This means that, other than the "type" property, how you structure your Action is completely up to yourself. You can define the "value" property directly in the Action object instead of defining it inside the "payload" property. In fact, you can define your own properties and values. But it is one of the recommended approaches to define all your properties within the "payload" property.

Reducers

Reducers are functions that specify how the State changes depending on the type and payload of the information dispatched by the Actions. These functions take in current State and Actions as input parameters, generate a new State after processing the information, and return this new State as output. Now, even though the State of our entire application is a single Store object, we might want to write multiple Reducers to modify this object. Redux gives you the flexibility to do that. Instead of writing a single Reducer function that deals with all the scenarios, you can write one small Reducer for each scenario. This will help us minimize code complexity.

> **Note**   Since all the Actions are executed sequentially, we will never face a
> scenario where multiple reducers are trying to modify the State at the same time.

The following is a code snippet for a sample Reducer function that returns the
initial state:

```
function sampleReducer(state, action) {
  return state
}
```

Let us create a basic example to understand the concept of Redux. Firstly, we will
install redux to our application by using the following command:

```
npm install redux --save
```

Once this is done, we will create two separate folders – "Actions" and "Reducers".
Let us modify our "index.js" file in the "pages" folder. We will have an input textbox, a
button, and a label. On click of the button, the State should be updated with the value
in the input textbox and the label should update itself with the State value. Some initial
value will be set for the State. Consider the following code:

Pages/index.js

```
import React from "react";
import '../style.css';

export default class extends React.Component {
  static async getInitialProps() {
    return { text: 'Initial label value.' }
  }

  constructor(props) {
    super(props);
    this.state = { text: props.text };
  }

  render() {
    return(
      <div>
```

121

```
        <h1>Redux Demo</h1>
        <br />
        <div className='center'>
          <input id='inputTextbox' type='text'>
          </input>
          <button type='button'
              onClick={this.GetUser}>
              Update Label
          </button>
        </div>
        <br />
        <p>{this.state.text}</p>
      </div>
    );
  }
}
```

If you visit this page in the browser, you will see an output similar to Figure 3-14.

Figure 3-14. *Redux Demo*

Note that we have just created a page with initial State value that the label consumes. We pass a static string as props using getInitialProps() method. In the constructor, we fetch the value of this prop and set it in the State. Note that we have not written any logic for changing updating the State. We will do that using Redux. But before we can do that, we will have to install some dependencies that will help us along the way. Use the following command to do the same:

```
npm install redux react-redux next-redux-wrapper redux-thunk redux-
devtools-extension --save
```

We have installed five new dependencies in total. Other dependencies that we already have are react, react-dom, next, axios, and @zeit/next-css. After installing the new dependencies, my "package.json" looks as follows:

package.json

```
{
  "name": "my-next-app",
  "version": "1.0.0",
  "description": "My Next.js Application",
  "main": "index.js",
  "scripts": {
    "start": "next"
  },
  "author": "Mohit Thakkar",
  "license": "ISC",
  "dependencies": {
    "@zeit/next-css": "^1.0.1",
    "axios": "^0.19.0",
    "next": "^9.1.6",
    "next-redux-wrapper": "^4.0.1",
    "react": "^16.12.0",
    "react-dom": "^16.12.0",
    "react-redux": "^7.1.3",
    "redux": "^4.0.5",
    "redux-devtools-extension": "^2.13.8",
    "redux-thunk": "^2.3.0"
  }
}
```

If you are creating a new application from scratch, make sure you update your "package.json" as mentioned in the preceding snippet and run "npm install" command from terminal to update the dependencies. It is time to create our first Action. I have created an "Actions" folder in the root directory of our application that will contain our action. Consider the following code:

Actions/actions.js

```
export const InitialState = {
    text: 'Initial label value.'
}

export const changeState = () => dispatch => {
 return dispatch({
  type:'ChangeLabel',
  text: document.getElementById('inputTextbox').value
 })
}
```

Here, we are defining an `InitialState`, which is a plain JavaScript object, and an Action that will update the State value with input text on button click. We will use the `InitialState` object directly in our Reducer function as well as while creating the Store for the first time. We will see that later. However, to update the State, we will have to dispatch an Action to the Reducer. To do so, we have created a method, `changeState()`, that will be called on button click. This method dispatches our Action.

For the Action that we are dispatching, we have defined a mandatory "`type`" property that determines the type of Action being performed and a "`text`" property which sends the new data to the reducer. It is time to create our Reducer function that will actually update the Store based on the data received from the Action. I have created a "Reducers" folder in the root directory of our application that will contain our reducer. Consider the following code:

Reducers/reducer.js

```
import { InitialState } from '../Actions/actions'

export const reducer = (state = InitialState, action) => {
  if (action.type == 'ChangeLabel') {
    return Object.assign({}, state, {
      text: action.text
    })
  }
  else {
    return state;
  }
}
```

As discussed earlier, Reducers take in two input parameters – current State and Action. While defining our Reducer, we assign "InitialState" as the default value for our first input parameter, state. If the reducer is triggered on an empty State, the initial state value defined in our "InitialState" object will be set to the State.

Note   "InitialState" is being imported from our Actions file and is the same object that we created earlier.

If the type of the Action is "ChangeLabel", the reducer will know that the State value needs to be updated with the data dispatched by the Action. In such a case, the Reducer function creates a new object, assigns the current State value to that object, and replaces the value of "text" property with the new value dispatched by the Action. This new object will be returned by the Reducer and will be considered as the new State of the application. React will automatically update the View as soon as it detects a change in the State. Hence, as soon as the Reducer is executed, the View will reflect the changes in State. We do not have any other Actions defined so we will just return the State object, as it is received, in case the type of the Action is not "ChangeLabel". It is now time to write the code that will create our Store for the first time. I have created a "Store" folder in the root directory of our application that will contain our Store initialization code. Consider the following code:

Store/store.js

```
import { createStore, applyMiddleware } from 'redux'
import thunkMiddleware from 'redux-thunk'
import { reducer } from '../Reducers/reducer'
import { InitialState } from '../Actions/actions.js'

export const initStore = (initialState = InitialState) => {
  return createStore(
    reducer,
    initialState,
    applyMiddleware(thunkMiddleware)
  )
}
```

Here, we have again used the "InitialState" object that we created in our Actions file, this time, to initialize the Store with the initial application State when it is being created for the first time. createStore() is a method provided by the "redux" library in order to create and initialize a Redux Store for the first time.

Note   There should only be a single store in your app.

We pass the following three parameters to the createStore() method:

- **reducer (Function)** – This is the Reducer function that we created for our Store. It returns the next application State, given the current state and an action.

- **initialState (any)** – This is the initial State of our application. It is a plain JavaScript object that we created in our Actions file.

- **enhancer (Function)** – You can optionally specify some functions that use third-party code to enhance your application. In our case, we have used the "thunkMiddleware" provided by the "redux-thunk" library. This middleware helps us write asynchronous logic that interacts with our Store. With a basic Redux Store without this Middleware, we will only be able to perform synchronous updates to the Store by dispatching an action. We will use applyMiddleware() provided by "redux" library to convert "thunkMiddleware" to an enhancer.

Note that the store is not yet created. We have just defined and exported the "initStore" function that can be invoked in order to create the Store.

You must have noticed that we have created everything that is required in order to perform State management using Redux. It is time to inject the Redux functionality in our application lifecycle. To do so, we will have to use "react-redux" library that we installed as one of the dependencies earlier. It is the official React binding for Redux. It helps React components read data from a Redux store and dispatch actions to the store to update the data. Since we need our State object to be available throughout the entire application, we will have to inject it in a component the rest of the components inherit from. This parent component can be referred to as a Higher-Order Component (HOC).

In Next.js, we can create a special component "_App.js" which wraps all the pages and can be used to share something that is common throughout the application. We will use this "_App" component to inject Redux to the application lifecycle. Add the "_App.js" file to the "Pages" folder with the following code:

Pages/_App.js

```
import React from 'react'
import { Provider } from 'react-redux'
import App from 'next/app'
import withRedux from 'next-redux-wrapper'
import { initStore } from '../Store/store'

export default withRedux(initStore)(
  class MyApp extends App {
    static async getInitialProps({ Component, ctx }){
      return {
        pageProps: Component.getInitialProps
          ? await Component.getInitialProps(ctx)
          : {},
      }
    }

    render() {

      const { Component, pageProps, store } = this.props

      return (
        <Provider store={store}>
          <Component {...pageProps} />
        </Provider>
      )
    }
  }
)
```

Here, we have created a component wrapped in a special `withRedux()()` wrapper provided by "next-redux-wrapper" library that we installed as one of the dependencies earlier. As the first input to this wrapper, we pass the method that creates the initial store, which in our case is "`initStore`" from "`Store/store.js`". The second input to this wrapper is our Higher-Order Component (HOC).

The component extends from "App" component provided by "Next" library. This is the component that Next.js uses in order to initialize Pages. Since we are overriding the default initialization of our Pages, we will have to write the `getInitialProps()` method in our Component and make it call the Page's `getInitialProps()` method. It takes in two arguments – "Component" and "ctx". "Component" is the Page Component and "ctx" is the context. If the Page's `getInitialProps()` method returns any data, we return that data from our HOC's `getInitialProps()` method, else we return an empty object.

Then we write the `render()` method of our HOC. We already have Component and PageProps in the Props object. Component is the Page Component for the Page that is being rendered, and PageProps is the Props that we have in that Page. Since we are wrapping our HOC in a Redux wrapper, the Store object is also created and passed down to the `render()` method when `getInitialProps()` method is executed. We have already specified the method which will create the initial Store. The same will be used to create the Store and pass it down to the HOC props. We will use the destructuring syntax to fetch the values for Component, pageProps, and store from the props object.

We will use the `<Provider>` component provided by "react-redux" library to wrap our Page Component. We will pass the Store object to this component which will be available to all our container components. Within this component, we will put the Page Component and pass the page props to it. Page Component will dynamically keep changing depending on the Page that is being rendered.

This is how you inject Redux to the Next.js lifecycle using a Higher-Order Component (HOC). Let us now consume our store in our index page and dispatch an Action on button click. You will have to make the following modification to the "index.js" file:

Pages/index.js

```
import React from "react";
import "../style.css";
import { connect } from 'react-redux'
import { bindActionCreators } from 'redux'
import { changeState } from '../Actions/actions'
```

```
class ReduxDemo extends React.Component {

  render() {
    return (
      <div>
        <h1>Redux Demo</h1>
        <br />
        <div className='center'>
          <input id='inputTextbox' type='text'>
          </input>
          <button type='button'
              onClick={this.props.changeState}>
              Update Label
          </button>
        </div>
        <br />
        <p>{this.props.text}</p>
      </div>
    );
  }
}

const mapDispatchToProps = dispatch => {
  return {
    changeState: bindActionCreators(changeState, dispatch)
  }
}

export default connect((state) => ({ text: state.text }),
mapDispatchToProps)(ReduxDemo)
```

You must have noticed that we have removed the getInitialProps() method from the code. That is because props will now be injected using a special "connect()()" wrapper provided by "react-redux" library. The first parameter contains State-related entities that you want to inject to the Page, and the second parameter is the Page itself. We are injecting the text property that resides in the state object. We are also injecting the method that is used to dispatch an Action to modify the Store object. We pass this method to the click event of the button by accessing it in the Page using "this.props. changeState". We also bind the label (<p>) to the "text" property of State object using "this.props.text". If you execute the application and visit the browser, you will see an output similar to Figure 3-14. The following is a sequential list of things happening when you run the application:

- The code written in "_App.js" gets executed when the page is first requested from the browser.

- redux-wrapper creates the Store object with initial values and injects it into the Page. initStore() method is used to create the Store for the first time. We have defined this method in "Store/store.js" and provided a reference to it in the HOC.

- The HOC in "_App.js" renders the Page Component. The control is now transferred to the code written in "Pages/index.js" file.

- "connect()()" wrapper injects the State data into the page via props. A method to update the State value is also passed as props. The page then renders like a normal Next.js Page. You will see the initial State value displayed on the label.

- As soon as you type some text and click the button, the changeState() method which is defined in "Actions/action.js" will be invoked.

- This method will dispatch an Action of type "ChangeLabel" with the text that you entered in the input textbox as data.

- The control will now be transferred to the Reducer method written at "Reducers/reducer.js". After checking the type of the Action, the Reducer will update the "text" property in State with the data dispatched by the Action.

- As soon as the State object is changed, React will re-render the Views and update all the fields whose data has been modified. Thus, the label on the UI that is bound to the "text" property of the State will be re-rendered and you will see the updated value on the UI.

Note that we are not using React's built-in State object anywhere directly in the Pages. All the State management here is done by Redux. That is it about working with Redux. Let us now learn about GraphQL and how it is used in a Next.js application.

Using GraphQL with Next.js

GraphQL is the query language for the APIs. It gives the client the power to ask for exactly what it requires. We can send a GraphQL query to the API and communicate to the server the exact fields that we require in the response. Look at Figure 3-15 for a better understanding.

Figure 3-15. *GraphQL Query Variables*

Figure 3-15 perfectly depicts the concept of GraphQL. An API might return multiple parameters, but we might not need all of those parameters for our application. In such cases, we can send the names of the parameters that we need as query variables and the API will return just that many parameters.

To understand the GraphQL in working, we will have to first create a regular API in our application and consume it. We will then see how to use GraphQL with that API. Next.js provides a straightforward solution to build APIs in your applications. All the files in the "Pages/api" folder are treated as API endpoints instead of Pages and can be consumed at "/api/*". For the API to work, you will have to export a request handler from your file, which is nothing but a function that takes in the following two parameters:

- **req** – An instance of the incoming request. You can use this object to identify the request type, input parameters, request headers, and URL from which the request is generated, among other things.

- **res** – An instance of the outgoing response. You can use this parameter to set the status code, headers, and data of the response.

Let us start with a basic Next.js application with just the index page. We will create the "Pages/api" folder and add our first API, "TestAPI.js" file with the following code:

Pages/api/TestAPI.js

```
const data = {
    name: 'Jhon Doe',
    address: '7th Avenue, Brooklyn',
    contact: '099251456',
    bloodgroup: 'A +ve',
    favouriteSnack: 'Hotdog',
    vehicle: 'Hyundai Tucson'
  }

export default (req, res) => {
    res.statusCode = 200
    res.setHeader('Content-Type', 'application/json')
    res.end(JSON.stringify(data))
}
```

What we are doing here is that we define a static data object and send it in response. We pass this data in the response's end( ) method. This method signals to the server that the response headers and the response body have been set and the server should consider this response as complete. We can consume this API by visiting the URL "http://localhost:*/api/testapi" in the browser. Alternatively, we can consume this API in our index page. Let us do it using the following code:

Pages/index.js

```
import React from "react";
import axios from 'axios';
import "../style.css";

export default class extends React.Component {
  static async getInitialProps() {
    try {
      const res = await axios.get('http://localhost:3000/api/testapi');
      return { data: res.data, error: null }
```

```
  } catch (e) {
    return { data: ", error: e }
  }
}
render() {
  return (
    <div>
      <h1>Hello, world!</h1>
      <table>
        {Object.keys(this.props.data).map((key, index) => (
          <tr key={index}>
            <td>{key}:</td>
            <td>{this.props.data[key]}</td>
          </tr>
        ))}
      </table>
    </div>
  );
}
}
```

We make the request to our API using the Axios library in the getInitialProps()
method of our Page. We then send the API response down to the rest of the Page as
Props. In the render method, we iterate over the data and render it to the browser.
Simple enough. We have created an API and consumed it. You shall see an output similar
to Figure 3-16.

Hello, world!	
name:	Jhon Doe
address:	7th Avenue, Brooklyn
contact:	099251456
bloodgroup:	A +ve
favouriteSnack:	Hotdog
vehicle:	Hyundai Tucson

Figure 3-16. *Next.js API Response*

Let us now consider a scenario where we only want the name and address fields from the API. Currently, you will have to get all the data from the API and then narrow down the fields you want on the consuming end. However, there is a better way to deal with this scenario using GraphQL. Let us install the GraphQL library to our application using the following command:

```
npm install graphql --save
```

We will now have to modify our API a little bit. We will define a schema for our data. This schema will specify the type of data that we will be returning from the API. We will then pass the schema, GraphQL query, and the data object to GraphQL which will filter the data for us as per the query received. Consider the following code for the API:

Pages/api/TestAPI.js

```
import { graphql, buildSchema } from 'graphql'

const schema = buildSchema(`
  type Query {
    name: String,
    address: String,
    contact: String,
    bloodgroup: String,
    favouriteSnack: String,
    vehicle: String
  }
`);

const data = {
    name: 'Jhon Doe',
    address: '7th Avenue, Brooklyn',
    contact: '099251456',
    bloodgroup: 'A +ve',
    favouriteSnack: 'Hotdog',
    vehicle: 'Hyundai Tucson'
}
```

```
export default async (req, res) => {
    const response = await graphql(schema, req.body.query, data);
    res.end(JSON.stringify(response.data))
}
```

buildSchema() is the method provided by GraphQL that helps us build our schema. It is a mapping of every property in our data object with its corresponding data type. We will fetch the GraphQL query from the request. We will then pass the schema, query, and data to the GraphQL and wait for the filtered response. Finally, we will send the response back to the user. In order to use GraphQL from the consuming end, all you need to do is add a "query" parameter along with your Axios request. Replace your Axios call in Index page to the following:

```
...
const res = await axios.get('http://localhost:3000/api/testapi',
{ data: { query: `{ name, address }` }});
...
```

If after all the changes, you visit the index page of our application, you will see an output similar to Figure 3-17. You will notice that only two fields will be displayed instead of all the fields that were displayed earlier. That is GraphQL at work in our application.

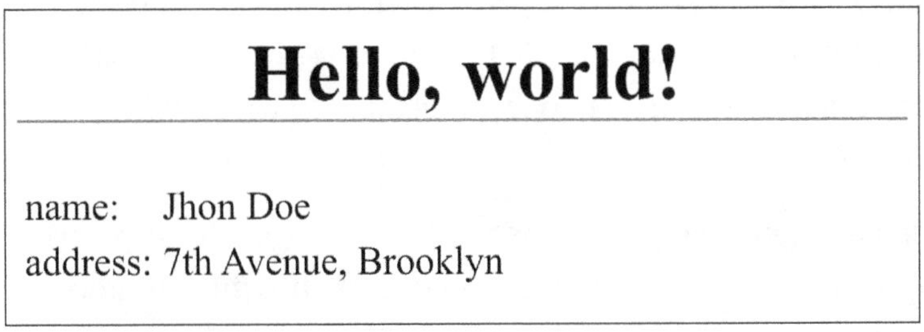

Hello, world!

name: Jhon Doe
address: 7th Avenue, Brooklyn

Figure 3-17. *GraphQL API Response*

That is it about GraphQL. With the end of this topic, we come to the end of the chapter. Let us summarize what we have learned.

Summary

- Next.js is a framework that helps us render applications on the server-side.

- It solves problems such as higher loading time, poor indexing capabilities, and security vulnerabilities that are associated with client-side rendering.

- It provides features such as hot reloading, page-based routing, automatic code splitting, page prefetching, hot module replacement, and server-side rendering.

- Next.js provides <Link> component that helps add links to our application. When we navigate to such links, no additional server requests will be made for the resource. This is due to the client-side routing capabilities of Next.js.

- Since it uses the History API, client-side routing in Next.js does not break the browser back button.

- We should add media files in the "static" folder in the root directory of our application. The best approach to add multimedia content to our application is to add URLs to such content in CSS files.

- Next.js provides JSS (CSS in JS) which allows us to define styles directly inside JSX code. We will have to use @zeit/next-css library (or any other CSS loader) in our application to write styling code in separate CSS files.

- We can use getInitialProps() method in our page to pass props to the component. We can make Axios API calls within this method to fetch data for our page from a remote server. Data passed as props can be used to initialize the State object in the constructor.

- Redux can be used in Next.js application in order to manage the State at an application level. It imitates the MVC architecture using Actions, Reducers, and Store.

- We use Higher-Order Component (HOC) to inject Redux into the Next.js lifecycle.

- GraphQL can be used in Next.js APIs to provide the client with the ability to query data for fields that they require in the response.

## CHAPTER 4

Adding Server-Side Rendering to Your React Application

In the previous chapter, we learned how to create a server-side application using the Next.js framework. However, we might want to create an application that is partially rendered on the client-side and partially on the server-side so that we can leverage the benefits of both client-side rendering and server-side rendering. In this chapter, we will create a client-side rendered React application and learn how to integrate server-side rendering into the application using Next.js framework. Along the way, we will also learn the importance of server-side rendering, styling our application, adding Bootstrap to our application, and some other topics. Mostly we will be using the things that we have already learned previously in order to create a functional application.

Importance of Server-Side Rendering

In the previous chapter, we discussed the problems associated with client-side rendering. The major problem is faced during the development of a single-page application (SPA). Although SPAs provide amazing user experience, all of it is browser-based. Instead of navigating from one page to another, the user stays on the same page and the content on the page is dynamically changed based on the user interaction. These changes are made by the browser using the JavaScript code that is written on the client-side.

While this is a great approach for changing the page once the application is up and running, it is not a recommended approach in order to load the application for the first time. Before the SPA is available for the user to interact with, there is a lot of processing

© Mohit Thakkar 2020
M. Thakkar, *Building React Apps with Server-Side Rendering*, https://doi.org/10.1007/978-1-4842-5869-9_4

required to be done by the browser. Also, multiple interactions are necessary between the web server and the user's browser. As you can see in Figure 4-1, when the user visits the application for the first time, a request is sent to the web server for the page. The server returns an HTML page which contains an empty root element (<div>) and some JavaScript code. The browser then sends more requests for data, stylesheets, script files, and other resources that it might require. Once all the resources are available to the browser, it processes the JavaScript code in order to make sure that the JSX code is correctly compiled, JSON data is loaded using REST API calls, all the events are bound, and the promises are fulfilled. Only then the page is made available to the user.

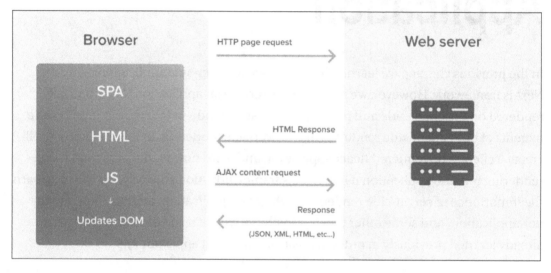

Figure 4-1.   *Client-Side Rendering of a Single-Page Application*

Note   Do not confuse the server used for client-side rendering with the server used for server-side rendering. The web server used here can be referred to as a "Thin Server". This is because, in the case of client-side rendering, all the logic is written in the form of JavaScript code which will be processed by the browser. The server acts as a pure data API and just delivers the JavaScript code to the browser. On the other hand, in the case of server-side rendering, the server processes all the logic and delivers a ready-to-render HTML page to the browser.

Adopting this approach might take a significant amount of time and result in poor user experience due to all the waiting-while-the-page-loads. This is where the server-side rendering steps in. We can prepare the initial page on the server-side and serve it to the user's browser which can then easily download the page and render it. This way, the initial application loading can be performed with a single web request. We have already learned how to use Next.js for server-side rendering in the previous chapter. Further in this chapter, we will see how to use both client-side rendering and server-side rendering to create a fully functional application. Let us start by creating a simple React application.

Building a Simple React App

We will create a simple application that displays the time on the browser. Use the following command to create a starter React application:

```
npx create-react-app my-app
```

Once the command is successfully executed, navigate to the "my-app" folder and delete all the files from the "src" directory except "index.js" file. Replace the code in "index.js" file with the following code:

```
import React from 'react';
import ReactDOM from 'react-dom';

ReactDOM.render(<h1>Hello from React.</h1>, document.getElementById
('root'));
```

On executing the application using "npm-start" command, you should see "Hello from React." printed on your browser window. Our starter React application is up and running. Let us now do this with the help of a React component.

Creating Functional React Component

Our component file will reside in the "src/Components" folder in the root directory of our application. Let us add the "App.js" file in the "Components" folder with the following code:

src/Components/App.js

```
import React from 'react';

function App(){
 return(
   <div>
     <h1>Hello from React.</h1>
   </div>
 );
}

export default App;
```

We will also need to make some changes to our "index.js" file in order to render the component instead of directly rendering the JSX code. Update the "index.js" file as per the following code:

src/index.js

```
import React from 'react';
import ReactDOM from 'react-dom';
import App from './Components/App';

ReactDOM.render(<App/>, document.getElementById('root'));
```

If you run the application and visit the browser, you should see "Hello from React." printed on the window. So far, we have not displayed the time on the browser. Let us do that using React props.

Passing Props to Functional React Component

We will simply pass the current time as props to the App component. The component will fetch the value from the props and render it to the browser. It is pretty simple. Let's do that by modifying our code as per the following:

src/Components/App.js

```
import React from 'react';
```

```
function App(props){
 return(
   <div>
     <h1>Time: {props.time}</h1>
   </div>
 );
}

export default App;
```

src/index.js

```
import React from 'react';
import ReactDOM from 'react-dom';
import App from './Components/App';

ReactDOM.render(
  <App time={new Date().toLocaleTimeString()}/>,
  document.getElementById('root')
);
```

As you can see, we have passed the time string as props to the component, which is then rendered to the browser. However, the React will not update the DOM yet because we have passed a static time string and React does not know yet when the time changes. To implement this functionality, we will have to write some JavaScript code to update the time stored in the "props" as the actual time passes. But we cannot do that because "props" are read-only. Hence, we will have to use the "state" functionality provided by the React lifecycle.

Converting Functional Component to Class Component

Let us convert our function component to a class component. Once we do that, we will be able to use React's "state" property in order to track changes to the time. The current directory structure of our application is shown in Figure 4-2.

Figure 4-2. *Current Directory Structure*

You will have to make the following changes in the code:

src/Components/App.js

```
import React from 'react';

class App extends React.Component {
  constructor(props) {
    super(props);
    this.state = {
      time: new Date().toLocaleTimeString()
    }
  }

  tick() {
    this.setState(() => {
      return ({
        time: new Date().toLocaleTimeString()
      });
    });
  }

  componentDidMount() {
    this.timer = setInterval(() => this.tick(), 1000);
  }
```

```
componentWillUnmount(){
    clearInterval(this.timer);
}

render() {
    return (
        <div>
            <h1>Time: {this.state.time}</h1>
        </div>
    );
}
}

export default App;
```

src/index.js

```
import React from 'react';
import ReactDOM from 'react-dom';
import App from './Components/App';

ReactDOM.render(<App/>, document.getElementById('root'));
```

As you can see, we are no longer passing the time string as props to the component. We set the state property to the current time in the constructor of our class component. Then we render it to the browser using the render method. The only difference here is that instead of fetching the value from "props", we now fetch it from the "state". Using the "state" property is necessary because as we discussed earlier, "props" are read-only and we cannot modify them directly.

Next, we had to find a way to update the state property with change in time. To do so, we created an interval using JavaScript's setInterval() method. We did this in the componentDidMount() method of the React lifecycle in order to make sure that the interval is set only once the component is mounted to the DOM.

Note   If you have created a function component, you can use React hooks to hook to the React lifecycle method `componentDidMount()`. You can go back to Chapter 2 of this book in order to see React hooks in working.

If you have created a function component, you can use React hooks to hook to the React lifecycle method `componentDidMount()`.

The interval calls the `tick()` method every one second which will eventually update the "`state`" object with the new time. As soon as the State is modified, React re-renders the view. Hence, the user sees a digital clock on the browser that ticks every second. We might want to clear the timer that we created when the component was mounted in the `componentWillUnmount()` method in order to avoid memory leaks in case the component is removed from the DOM.

That is it. Our application is completely functional. We have achieved this entirely by the approach of client-side rendering using React. Let us see how to add server-side rendering to this application using Next.js framework.

Using Next.js for Server-Side Rendering

In order to use Next.js framework for server-side rendering, we will have to install it to our application using the following command:

```
npm install next --save
```

Once installed, we will need to change the "scripts" section in our "package.json" file as per the following:

```
...
"scripts": {
    "start": "next",
    "build": "next build",
    "test": "echo \"Error: no test specified\" && exit 1"
  }
...
```

If you try to launch the application, you will run into an error stating that the "Pages" directory is not found. We will have to create it and add our "app.js" file to that directory because that is where Next.js loads the pages from. We can delete our "index.js" file (which contains the code for rendering our components) because Next.js will take care of the rendering for us. We can also delete the "src" and "public" folders because they are of no use to us. For simplicity, we can rename "app.js" file in the "Pages" directory to "index.js" because, as we learned in the previous chapter, Next.js follows a page-based routing and it looks for "index.js" page on application startup. Now if you launch the application, you will see an identical timer to the one created using client-side rendering. If you want to verify that the content is being rendered on the server-side, you can right-click the page and view the page source. You will notice the presence of HTML code for the timer instead of an empty <div> tag. This tells us that the timer is not being generated using client-side JavaScript but is being generated on the server-side. However, the page is not being reloaded every second. This means that the update in the state is being handled by React on the client-side. This is exactly as we wanted it to be, initial application rendering on the server-side and other DOM changes on the client-side. Now that our application is up and running, let us add some styling to it.

Adding CSS to Next.js

As discussed in the previous chapter, we will have to use an external CSS loader in order to add styling to our Next.js application. Let us install "@zeit/next-css" module to our application which will act as a CSS loader. Use the following command:

```
npm install @zeit/next-css --save
```

Once installed, we will have to add a config file "next.config.js" to the root of our application with the following code:

next.config.js

```
const withCSS = require('@zeit/next-css')
module.exports = withCSS({})
```

This config file acts as an entry point to the webpack configuration of our application that is, by default, hidden by the Next.js framework. Once configured, we can create a stylesheet for our application and import it to our page along with other imports. Consider the following stylesheet that I have created in the "Resources" folder:

Resources/style.css

```
body{
    margin-top: 45vh;
    text-align: center;
}

h1{
    display:inline-block;
    border: 5px solid black;
    border-radius: 10px;
    padding: 10px;
}
```

The current directory structure of our application is shown in Figure 4-3.

Figure 4-3. *Current Directory Structure*

I have imported it to our Index page using the following statement:

```
import '../Resources/style.css'
```

If you launch the application and visit the browser, you shall see an output similar to Figure 4-4.

```
Time: 15:22:32
```

Figure 4-4. *Digital Clock Using Next.js and React*

We can also add Bootstrap to our application in order to add responsiveness to our application. Let us see how to do that.

Integrating Bootstrap to Your App

In order to use bootstrap, we will have to first install it to our application using the following command:

```
npm install --save bootstrap
```

On the successful execution of this command, you shall see the bootstrap module added to our "node_modules" folder. Since we have already installed the Zeit CSS loader and configured it in our application, we will directly be able to import the bootstrap CSS file in our page and use the classes provided by the Bootstrap framework. Refer to the following code in order to understand how it is done:

Note   If you need to apply CSS globally in your application, you should create a Higher-Order Component (HOC) that wraps all your components and then import the CSS file in the HOC. This will spare you the trouble of having to import CSS file in every component that you create. We learned how to create a HOC in the previous chapter while learning about Reducers in Redux. If you do not remember, you can go back and have a look.

Pages/index.js

```
import React from 'react';
import 'bootstrap/dist/css/bootstrap.min.css';
```

```
class App extends React.Component {
  constructor(props) {
    super(props);
    ...
  }

  tick() {
    ...
  }

  componentDidMount() {
    ...
  }

  componentWillUnmount() {
    ...
  }

  render() {
    return (
      <div>
        <div className="jumbotron text-center">
          <h1>Digital Clock with React, Next.js, and Bootstrap</h1>
        </div>
        <div className="text-center">
          <p>Time: {this.state.time}</p>
        </div>
      </div>
    );
  }
}

export default App;
```

We have completely removed our custom stylesheet "style.css" from our page and replaced it with the bootstrap stylesheet. We have used two classes from bootstrap – "jumbotron", which allows us to define a header section for our application, and "text-center", which makes sure that the content is center aligned. The output of the preceding code should be similar to Figure 4-5.

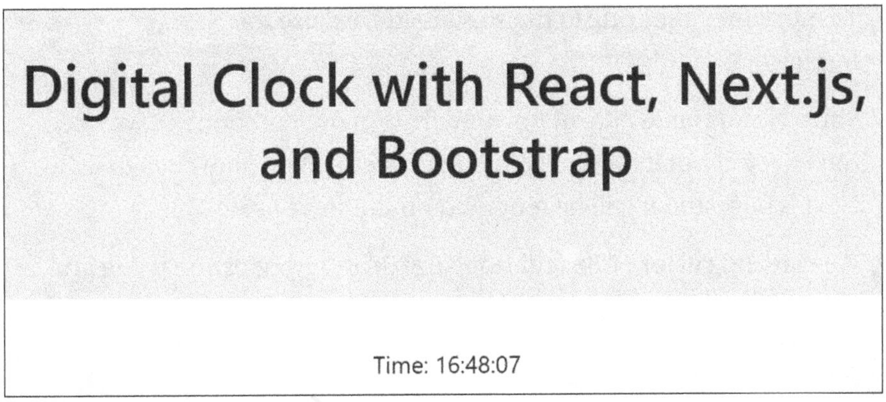

Digital Clock with React, Next.js, and Bootstrap

Time: 16:48:07

Figure 4-5. *Digital Clock with Bootstrap*

With this, we come to the end of this chapter. You can add some more pages to the application, establish links between them, and play around with the bootstrap classes. The more you explore, the more you will learn. Let us summarize what we have learned in this chapter.

Summary

- Server-side rendering is very useful while loading a single-page application for the first time. It results in better user experience due to lesser wait time. Subsequent DOM changes can be made on the client-side.

- A simple client-side React application can be created using a function component. We can pass props to the component, and it can then render the prop data to the browser window.

- Since props are read-only, we cannot directly modify them. A better approach is to use React's state object if we are dealing with props that need to be modified during the page lifecycle.

- componentDidMount() is a React lifecycle method that can be used by class components to trigger events when the component is mounted to the DOM. In our case, we have used this method to modify the state object with updated time every second.

- To move the rendering to the server-side, we use the Next.js framework.

- Since Next.js takes care of the rendering of our component, we need not worry about it. We can simply move our client-side code to a Next.js page and it will be rendered on the server-side.

- We can add custom CSS and Bootstrap in our application using an external loader.

CHAPTER 5

Unit Testing Using Jest

In previous chapters, we learned how to create web applications using libraries such as React and Next.js. We now know how to develop an application using these libraries. What next?

Once an application is developed, it is important for us to know that it works as expected. To do so, we can write automated unit tests to verify that every component of our application is appropriately doing its job. That is exactly what we are going to learn in this chapter. We will use the Jest framework to perform unit testing on our React application.

Note As a developer, writing unit tests might seem to be delivering very minimal value while adding a lot of work to your already cramped schedule. However, it will help you reduce your workload in the long run when your application scales up in size, providing a very effective way to detect errors and loopholes in your code.

There are many other JavaScript testing frameworks in the market such as Mocha and Jasmine. However, we will go with the Jest framework due to its increasing popularity and utility. We will learn how to install and set up Jest in our application, then we will create a basic unit test to familiarize ourselves with the concept of Jest, and eventually, we will learn about Matchers and Enzymes that will help us test our React component. Let us start by setting up the Jest framework.

© Mohit Thakkar 2020
M. Thakkar, *Building React Apps with Server-Side Rendering*, https://doi.org/10.1007/978-1-4842-5869-9_5

Setting Up Jest

Jest (`https://jestjs.io/`) is a JavaScript testing framework that we will use in order to test our React application. Let us start by creating our application directory, "jest-testing-app". Navigate to the directory and execute the "`npm init`" command to create a package.json file in the directory. Make sure that Node is installed in your system for the command to work. Once successfully executed, you will see a "package.json" file with the following code:

```
{
  "name": "jest-testing-app",
  "version": "1.0.0",
  "description": "My Jest Application",
  "main": "index.js",
  "scripts": {
    "test": "jest"
  },
  "author": "Mohit Thakkar",
  "license": "ISC"
}
```

The values might differ if you have specified a different set of values during initialization. Since we will be using Jest for testing, make sure that you specify "jest" as the value for the "test" attribute in the "scripts" section. We will now install Jest to our application using the following command:

```
npm install jest --save
```

Once installed, you will see the following dependency section added to your "package.json" file:

```
"dependencies": {
  "jest": "^24.9.0"
}
```

That's it. Jest is now successfully installed. Let us write our first test using Jest.

Writing Your First Test Using Jest

Let us first create a simple JavaScript file that contains some basic functions. I have added a file called "functions.js" to the root directory of our application with the following code:

functions.js

```
const functions = {
    add: (n1, n2) => n1 + n2
}

module.exports = functions
```

This file contains a simple "add" function that takes in two numbers as input and returns their sum as output. Note that we have used simple JavaScript syntax to export the list of functions as a module. Avoid using ES6 syntax because Jest expects the files to be plain JavaScript while they are imported. Now that we have created a JavaScript function, let us test it using Jest. We will add our test files in the "tests" directory. It is a good practice to name the test file as the same JavaScript file you are testing, with ".test.js" suffix. Consider the following test file that contains the code to test the "add" function:

tests/function.test.js

```
functions = require('../functions.js')

test('Test Add Function',()=>{
    expect(functions.add(2,3)).toBe(5)
})
```

That is it. We have created our first test using Jest framework. Let us understand what is happening here:

- In the code for the test, we simply call the "test()" function that takes in two input parameters – the first one being a description of the test and the second one being the actual test function.

- In the test function, we use the "expect()" function that takes in the function that we are testing and evaluates it, in our case, the "add()" function.

- We import the list of functions from "`functions.js`" using JavaScript's "`require()`" method because in order to call the "`add()`" function, we will have to import it from the file in which it is defined.

- We use a Matcher, in this case, the "`toBe()`" function, on the "`expect()`" function in order to compare the evaluated value with the expected value. We pass the expected value as an input parameter to the Matcher. We will learn more about Matchers in the next topic.

Use the following command to run your tests:

```
npm test
```

On successful execution of the command, you will see the summary of test execution in the terminal, as shown in Figure 5-1.

```
PASS  tests/functions.test.js
  √ Test Add Function (4ms)

Test Suites: 1 passed, 1 total
Tests:       1 passed, 1 total
Snapshots:   0 total
Time:        3.211s
Ran all test suites.
```

Figure 5-1. *First Test Using Jest (Success)*

Note   It is possible to write multiple tests in a single file.

The "Test Suites" denotes the number of test files, whereas the "Tests" denotes the combined number of tests in those files. In the preceding example, if we change the expected value to something else, let us say "4", the test execution will fail. Let us try that. Consider the following changes to "function.test.js" file:

tests/function.test.js

```
functions = require('../functions.js')

test('Test Add Function',()=>{
    expect(functions.add(2,3)).toBe(4)
})
```

Now, if you run the "npm test" command, you will see in the terminal that the test execution has failed. As shown in Figure 5-2, you will also see the reason due to which the test execution failed, in this case, received value not being equal to the expected value. You will also see both received and expected values in the test execution summary.

```
FAIL  tests/functions.test.js
  × Test Add Function (8ms)

  ● Test Add Function

    expect(received).toBe(expected) // Object.is equality

    Expected: 4
    Received: 5

      2 |
      3 | test('Test Add Function',()=>{
    > 4 |      expect(functions.add(2,3)).toBe(4)
        |                                 ^
      5 | })

      at Object.<anonymous>.test (tests/functions.test.js:4:32)

Test Suites: 1 failed, 1 total
Tests:       1 failed, 1 total
Snapshots:   0 total
Time:        3.738s
Ran all test suites.
npm ERR! Test failed.  See above for more details.
```

Figure 5-2. *First Test Using Jest (Failure)*

Now that we have learned how to write tests for JavaScript functions using Jest, let us delve a little deeper and learn about different Matchers that we can use for testing our code.

Matchers

Matchers are function used by Jest in order to compare the evaluated value with the expected value. In the previous example, we used the "toBe()" Matcher provided by Jest. Note that we use the "expect()" function in order to evaluate the actual value. This function returns an expectation object on which we call our Matcher function to compare it with the expected value. Let us have a look at all the Matchers that are provided by Jest.

Common Matchers

The following are some of the general-purpose Matchers that are used very commonly:

- **toBe(expectedValue)** – This is the exact equality matcher. It checks if the value returned by the "expect()" function exactly matches the "expectedValue".

- **toEqual(expectedValue)** – This is similar to the "toBe()" matcher, except the fact that it is used to compare the value of an object. It recursively checks every property of an object.

Let us look at an example in order to understand the common Matchers in working. Consider the following changes to "functions.test.js" file:

tests/functions.test.js

```
functions = require('../functions.js')

test('toBe Demo',()=>{
  expect(functions.add(2,3)).toBe(5)
})

test('toEqual Demo',()=>{
  var data = {name:'Mohit'}
  data['country'] = 'India'
  expect(data).toEqual({
    name:'Mohit',
    country:'India'
  })
})
```

158

To demonstrate the utility of the "toBe()" Matcher, we use the same "add()" function that we tested during the previous example. The function returns "5" and the "toBe()" Matcher asserts it to be true since it is the value that we are expecting.

For "toEqual()" Matcher, we define a new test, "toEqual Demo". We define a "data" object with one property and then add a new property to the object. We now pass the "data" object to the "expect()" function and use the "toEqual()" Matcher in order to compare it with the expected output. Since both values match, Jest will assert the test to be true. The output of the preceding example should be similar to Figure 5-3.

```
PASS  tests/functions.test.js
  √ toBe Demo (3ms)
  √ toEqual Demo (2ms)

Test Suites: 1 passed, 1 total
Tests:       2 passed, 2 total
Snapshots:   0 total
Time:        3.819s
Ran all test suites.
```

Figure 5-3. *Common Matchers in Jest*

If you want to try more scenarios, you can change the expected value in the preceding example and notice that the test fails.

Note   You can use the "Jest" extension by "Orts" if you are using Visual Studio Code editor. It provides IntelliSense for Jest and is also very helpful in debugging tests that you write.

Truth Matchers

These are the Matchers that let you check if the evaluated value is null, undefined, defined, true, or false. You need not pass any input parameters to these Matchers:

- **toBeNull()** – Matches null values

- **toBeUndefined()** – Matches values that are undefined

- **toBeDefined()** – Matches values that are not undefined

- **toBeTruthy()** – Matches the values that evaluate to true

- **toBeFalsy()** – Matches the values that evaluate to false

Let us look at an example in order to understand truth Matchers in working. The following new tests need to be added to the "functions.test.js" file:

tests/functions.test.js

```
...
test('truth of null', () => {
    const n = null;
    expect(n).toBeNull();
    expect(n).toBeDefined();
    expect(n).not.toBeUndefined();
    expect(n).not.toBeTruthy();
    expect(n).toBeFalsy();
});

test('truth of zero', () => {
    const n = 0;
    expect(n).not.toBeNull();
    expect(n).toBeDefined();
    expect(n).not.toBeUndefined();
    expect(n).not.toBeTruthy();
    expect(n).toBeFalsy();
});
...
```

We have written two new tests in the preceding example, one to test the truthiness of "null" and the other to check the truthiness of the number zero. The null value should evaluate to null, defined, and not true. On the other hand, the number zero should evaluate to not null, defined, and false. If you use any number other than zero, it should evaluate to true.

Note that we have used "not" keyword to negate certain Matchers. So, if an expression evaluates to "false", we can use the "not" keyword with "toBeTruthy()" Matcher in order to assert it. The output of the preceding example should be similar to Figure 5-4.

```
PASS   tests/functions.test.js
  √ toBe Demo (3ms)
  √ toEqual Demo (2ms)
  √ truth of null (2ms)
  √ truth of zero (1ms)

Test Suites: 1 passed, 1 total
Tests:       4 passed, 4 total
Snapshots:   0 total
Time:        4.58s
Ran all test suites.
```

Figure 5-4. *Truth Matchers in Jest*

Comparison Matchers

These are the Matchers that allow you to compare the actual value to another value. The value to which you want to compare the actual value is to be passed as an input parameter to the comparison Matcher:

- **toBeGreaterThan(value)** – Asserts if the actual value is greater than the provided value.

- **toBeGreaterThanOrEqual(value)** – Asserts if the actual value is greater than or equal to the provided value.

- **toBeLessThan(value)** – Asserts if the actual value is less than the provided value.

- **toBeLessThanOrEqual(value)** – Asserts if the actual value is less than or equal to the provided value.

- **toBeCloseTo(value)** – Asserts if the actual value is close to the provided value. This is specially used while dealing with floating-point values. In such cases, the precision of the expected value and the actual value might differ, so the "toBe()" Matcher (exact equality) would not work.

Let us look at an example in order to understand comparison Matchers in working. The following are the new tests added to the "functions.test.js" file:

161

tests/functions.test.js

```
...
test('comparison', () => {
  const value = 4 + 0.2;
  expect(value).toBeGreaterThan(3);
  expect(value).toBeGreaterThanOrEqual(3.5);
  expect(value).toBeLessThan(5);
  expect(value).toBeLessThanOrEqual(4.5);
  expect(value).toBeCloseTo(4.2);
});
...
```

The actual value in the preceding example will evaluate to "4.2". This is compared with multiple values using the comparison Matchers. Note that in order to assert the exact value, we have used the "toBeCloseTo()" Matcher instead of "toBe()" matcher due to a likely difference in precision. The output of the preceding example should be similar to Figure 5-5.

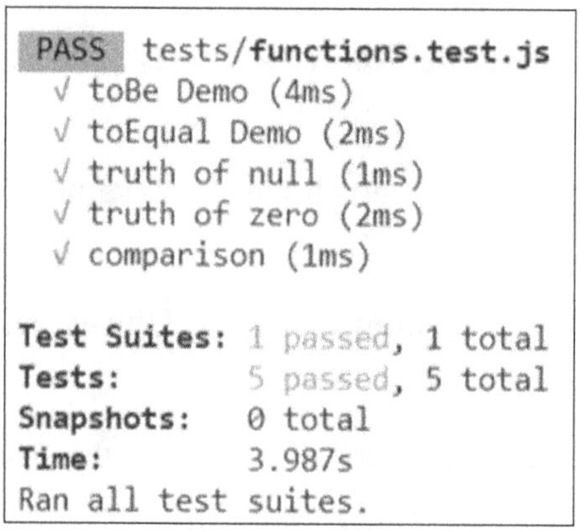

```
PASS  tests/functions.test.js
 √ toBe Demo (4ms)
 √ toEqual Demo (2ms)
 √ truth of null (1ms)
 √ truth of zero (2ms)
 √ comparison (1ms)

Test Suites: 1 passed, 1 total
Tests:       5 passed, 5 total
Snapshots:   0 total
Time:        3.987s
Ran all test suites.
```

Figure 5-5. *Comparison Matchers in Jest*

String Matcher

This Matcher is used to compare the actual value with a regular expression:

- **toMatch(regex)** – Asserts if the computed string matches the provided regular expression

Consider the following example:

tests/functions.test.js

```
...
test('String Matcher', () => {
  expect('Mohit is a Developer').toMatch(/Mohit/);
});
...
```

The preceding test asserts that the substring "Mohit" exists in the computed string. The output should be similar to Figure 5-6.

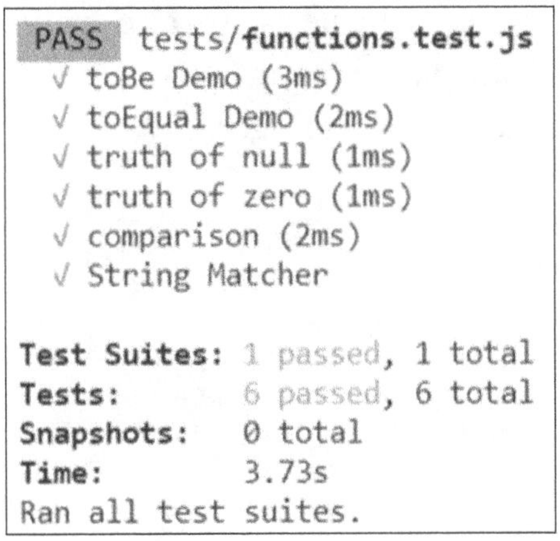

```
PASS  tests/functions.test.js
  √ toBe Demo (3ms)
  √ toEqual Demo (2ms)
  √ truth of null (1ms)
  √ truth of zero (1ms)
  √ comparison (2ms)
  √ String Matcher

Test Suites: 1 passed, 1 total
Tests:       6 passed, 6 total
Snapshots:   0 total
Time:        3.73s
Ran all test suites.
```

Figure 5-6. *String Matcher in Jest*

Matcher for Iterables

This Matcher is used to check if an item exists in an iterable such as a List or an Array:

- **toContain(item)** – Asserts if the computed iterable contains the provided item

Consider the following example:

tests/functions.test.js

```
...
const countries = [
  'India',
  'United Kingdom',
```

```
  'United States',
  'Japan',
  'Canada',
];

test('Matcher for Iterables', () => {
  expect(countries).toContain('India');
  expect(new Set(countries)).toContain('Canada');
});
...
```

In the preceding test, we define a list of countries and use the "toContain()" Matcher to check if "India" is present in the list. We also convert the list to a different iterable, a Set, and check if "Canada" is present in the new Set. Both the Matchers should assert true. The output should be similar to Figure 5-7.

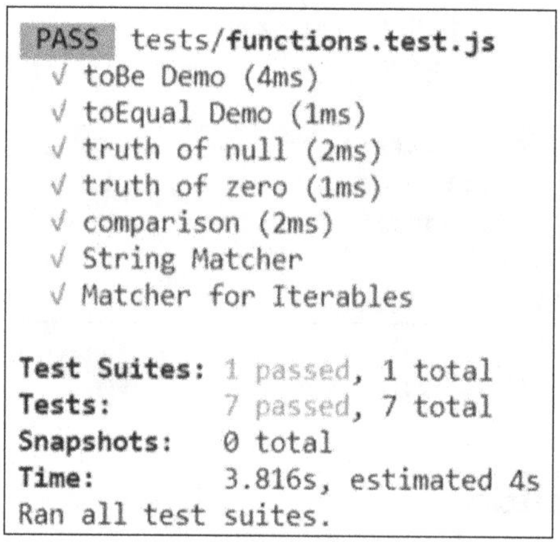

```
PASS  tests/functions.test.js
  √ toBe Demo (4ms)
  √ toEqual Demo (1ms)
  √ truth of null (2ms)
  √ truth of zero (1ms)
  √ comparison (2ms)
  √ String Matcher
  √ Matcher for Iterables


Test Suites: 1 passed, 1 total
Tests:       7 passed, 7 total
Snapshots:   0 total
Time:        3.816s, estimated 4s
Ran all test suites.
```

Figure 5-7. *Iterable Matchers in Jest*

Exception Matcher

This Matcher is used to assert if a particular exception is thrown while evaluating a particular piece of code:

- **toThrow(expectedException)** – Asserts if the evaluated piece of code throws the given exception

To test this Matcher, we will go back to our "function.js" file and define a function that throws an error. We will then add a test in the "functions.test.js" file which will invoke the function and assert the exception. Consider the following example:

function.js

```
const functions = {
    add: (n1, n2) => n1 + n2,
    invalidOperation: () => {
      throw new Error('Operation not allowed!')
    }
}

module.exports = functions
```

tests/functions.test.js

```
functions = require('../functions.js')
...
test('Exception Matcher', () => {
  expect(functions.invalidOperation)
    .toThrow(Error);

  expect(functions.invalidOperation)
    .toThrow('Operation not allowed!');

  expect(functions.invalidOperation)
    .toThrow(/not allowed/);
});
...
```

In the preceding example, we have invoked the function that throws an error and matched the computed value to the expected value using the "toThrow()" matcher. Note that we can either compare it to a generic error object, a specific string that the error returns, or a regular expression. The output of the preceding example should be similar to Figure 5-8.

```
PASS  tests/functions.test.js
  √ toBe Demo (4ms)
  √ toEqual Demo (1ms)
  √ truth of null (2ms)
  √ truth of zero (7ms)
  √ comparison (2ms)
  √ String Matcher
  √ Matcher for Iterables
  √ Exception Matcher (5ms)

Test Suites: 1 passed, 1 total
Tests:       8 passed, 8 total
Snapshots:   0 total
Time:        4.045s
Ran all test suites.
```

Figure 5-8. *Exception Matcher in Jest*

That is it. We have covered most of the commonly used Jest Matchers. Let us now learn how to test our React components using what we have learned so far.

Testing a React Component Using Jest and Enzyme

In order to test a React component, we will have to first create a React component. Let us create a starter React application using the following command:

```
npx create-react-app react-jest-app
```

Once the starter application is created, you can delete all the files that are not necessary. I have deleted all the files from the "src" folder except "index.js" and all the files from the "public" folder except "index.html" and "favicon.ico". I have also cleaned up the "index.html" file. The following is the code for your reference:

public/index.html

```
<!DOCTYPE html>
<html lang="en">
  <head>
    <meta charset="utf-8" />
    <link rel="icon"
        href="%PUBLIC_URL%/favicon.ico" />
    <title>React App</title>
```

```
  </head>
  <body>
    <noscript>
      You need to enable JavaScript to run this app.
    </noscript>
    <div id="root"></div>
  </body>
</html>
```

Now that we have cleaned up our starter application, let us add our List component in the "src" folder. Consider the following code:

src/List.js

```
import React from 'react';

function List(props) {
  const { items } = props;
  if (!items.length) {
      return(
        <span className="empty-message">
          No items in list
        </span>;
      );
  }

  return (
    <ul className="list-items">
      {items.map(item =>
        <li key={item} className="item">{item}</li>
      )}
    </ul>
  );
}

export default List;
```

The preceding code is for a simple function component that fetches the items from the props and displays them as a list. Now that our component is created, we might want to instruct the "index.js" file to render it on the browser. Consider the following code for "index.js" file:

src/index.js

```
import React from 'react';
import ReactDOM from 'react-dom';
import List from './List';

const data = ['one', 'two', 'three']
ReactDOM.render(<List items={data} />, document.getElementById('root'));
```

If you launch the application and visit the browser window, you should see an output similar to Figure 5-9.

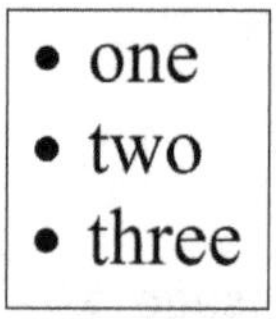

- one
- two
- three

Figure 5-9. *List Component Using React*

Now that we have created a React component, let us learn how to test it. Let us first install the Jest framework using the following command:

```
npm install jest@24.9.0 --save
```

Note   We have installed a specific version of the Jest framework. This is because applications initialized using "create-react-app" command have a dependency on this version of Jest. If your version of the Jest framework does not match the required version, you will get an error during the launch of the application mentioning the version that you need. You can resolve the error by installing the version that the application requires.

After installing the Jest framework, you will also have to add the test script in "package.json" file as per the following code:

package.json

```
{
  ...
  "scripts": {
    ...
    "test": "jest",
    ...
  },
  ...
}
```

While testing simple JavaScript functions, we used to simply invoke the functions in our tests and compare the evaluated value to the expected value using Jest Matchers. But you might wonder what to do in case of a react component because we cannot just invoke a component.

We will do exactly what React does. We will render the component on to the DOM, but it won't be the actual browser DOM; it will be a representational DOM created by a framework called Enzyme. This framework helps us simulate the runtime environment so that we can test our components. Let us install the dependencies for Enzyme framework using the following command:

```
npm install enzyme enzyme-adapter-react-16 –save
```

Note that we have also installed an adapter along with the Enzyme framework that corresponds to the version of React that we are using. We will have to configure this adapter in Enzyme before we can use the framework. To do so, we will create an "enzyme.js" file in the root directory of our application and add the following configuration code to it:

enzyme.js

```
import Enzyme, { configure, shallow, mount } from 'enzyme';
import Adapter from 'enzyme-adapter-react-16';

configure({ adapter: new Adapter() });
export { shallow, mount };
export default Enzyme;
```

What we are doing in the preceding code is that we import "Enzyme" and "configure" from the Enzyme framework and the "Adapter" from the Enzyme Adapter. We then use the "`configure()`" method provided by the Enzyme framework to set the Adapter for the instance of the Enzyme that we will be using. After configuring Enzyme, we simply export it. We also import shallow and mount from the Enzyme framework and export them as they are. These are the methods that we will be using to render our React components for testing. To conclude, all the entities of the Enzyme that we need for our testing will now be imported from the file "enzyme.js" instead of directly being imported from the framework. If you try to import the modules directly from the Enzyme framework installation folder, you might run into an error because they are not configured with the Adapter.

Now that everything is configured, let us write our test for the List component. Let us write the test in "List.test.js" file in the "src" folder. Refer to the following code:

src/List.test.js

```
import React from "react";
import { shallow, mount } from '../enzyme';

import List from './List';

test('List Component Test', () => {
  const items = ['one', 'two', 'three'];
  const wrapperShallow = shallow(<List items={items} />);
  const wrapperFull = mount(<List items={items} />);

  console.log(wrapperFull.debug());

  expect(wrapperShallow.find('.list-items'))
    .toBeDefined();
  expect(wrapperShallow.find('.item'))
    .toHaveLength(items.length);

  expect(wrapperFull.find('.list-items'))
    .toBeDefined();
  expect(wrapperFull.find('.item'))
    .toHaveLength(items.length);
})
```

Note that we have used two different methods to render our component – shallow and mount. Let us understand the difference between the two. As the name suggests, the "shallow()" method limits the scope of rendering to the specified component and does not render its children components. On the other hand, the "mount()" method renders the entire tree of components. In this case, we do not have any children components so the rendering would be the same in both cases.

We pass three items to the component for rendering. The rest of the syntax is similar to the one in which we tested the JavaScript functions. The "shallow()" and "mount()" methods return a React wrapper. If you want to see what the wrapper contains, you can invoke the "debug()" method on the wrapper and log the output to the console, just like we did in the preceding code. You can see in the output of the preceding test, shown in Figure 5-10, that the entire HTML rendering of our component is logged on the console. We can use the "find()" method on this wrapper to look for elements in the rendered code. We can pass multiple kinds of selectors to the "find()" method. This should be done in the "expect()" method so that we can use Matchers for the assertion. In the preceding example, we have used the class selector in order to evaluate and assert the existence and length of the list items. The following are some other selectors that you can use:

ID Selector

```
wrapper.find('#item1')
```

Combination of Tag and Class

```
wrapper.find('div.item')
```

Combination of Tag and ID

```
wrapper.find('div#item1')
```

Property Selector

```
wrapper.find('[htmlFor="checkbox"]')
```

If you execute the test using the "npm test" command, you might still get an error regarding an unexpected token while rendering. This is because Enzyme does not understand the JSX code that we have supplied to the "shallow()" and "mount()" methods. We will have to install and configure a babel transformer plugin that will transform the JSX code for us. Install it using the following command:

```
npm install babel-plugin-transform-export-extensions --save
```

Also, we need to create a ".babelrc" file in the root directory of our application and provide the following configurations:

.babelrc

```
{
  "env": {
    "test": {
      "presets": ["@babel/preset-env",
                  "@babel/preset-react"],
      "plugins": ["transform-export-extensions"],
      "only": [
        "./**/*.js",
        "node_modules/jest-runtime"
      ]
    }
  }
}
```

If you run the test after installing and configuring the babel transform plugin, the test should successfully run and the output should be similar to Figure 5-10.

```
PASS  src/List.test.js
  √ List Component Test (65ms)

  console.log src/List.test.js:11
    <List items={{...}}>
      <ul className="list-items">
        <li className="item">
          one
        </li>
        <li className="item">
          two
        </li>
        <li className="item">
          three
        </li>
      </ul>
    </List>

Test Suites: 1 passed, 1 total
Tests:       1 passed, 1 total
Snapshots:   0 total
Time:        5.33s, estimated 9s
Ran all test suites.
```

Figure 5-10. *Testing List Component Using Jest*

That is it. We have successfully tested our React component using Jest and Enzyme. With the end of this topic, we come to the end of this chapter.

Let us summarize what we have learned.

Summary

- Jest is a test framework that can be used to test applications built using JavaScript.

- It is good practice to suffix your test files with ".test.js".

- While testing, the "expect()" method is used to evaluate a JavaScript function or specify a value that needs to be tested.

- Jest provides various Matchers that can be used on the "expect()" method to assert if the computed value matches the expected value.

- Since React components cannot be directly invoked like functions, we will have to use the Enzyme framework that provides us the functionality to render components on a representational DOM that is created for testing.

- The Enzyme framework provides two main methods for rendering a component – shallow() and mount().

- We can use selectors with "find()" method to look for specific content within the rendered component.

## CHAPTER 6

Deploying Your App to a Server

In the previous chapters, we have learned how to build and test our React application. Once we have done that, we might want to know how our application performs in a production environment. That is when deployment comes into the picture.

In this chapter, we will learn how to deploy our application using Docker containers. Let us get started by learning about the deployment process.

Deployment Process

So far, we have executed our application locally. However, in order to deploy our application to a production server, we need to follow certain steps. Consider the following process:

- Firstly, we need to configure the application by setting some environment variables in our code. This will help the application identify the environment in which it is running and behave accordingly.

- We will then need to install Docker on our system to containerize our application.

- Once the configuration is done and Docker is installed, we need to build a Docker image of our application. We will learn more about Docker in the subsequent topics of the chapter.

- Once we know that the Docker image works fine locally, we can deploy it to a public-facing server.

175

© Mohit Thakkar 2020
M. Thakkar, *Building React Apps with Server-Side Rendering*, https://doi.org/10.1007/978-1-4842-5869-9_6

Now that we are aware of the deployment process, let us start by setting up the configuration for our application. If you do not follow or are confused about the process that we just discussed, do not worry. You will get a better understanding once we discuss each step in detail.

Setting Up Environment Variables

Environment variables are key-value pairs that can be read by our React application in order to configure the values on the runtime depending on the environment that the application is running in. It facilitates the dynamic behavior of the application. To understand this in working, we will use the GraphQL application that we developed in Chapter 3. The following is the code for your reference:

package.json

```json
{
  "name": "my-next-app",
  "version": "1.0.0",
  "description": "My Next.js Application",
  "main": "index.js",
  "scripts": {
    "start": "next"
  },
  "author": "Mohit Thakkar",
  "license": "ISC",
  "dependencies": {
    "@zeit/next-css": "^1.0.1",
    "axios": "^0.19.0",
    "graphql": "^14.5.8",
    "next": "^9.1.6",
    "react": "^16.12.0",
    "react-dom": "^16.12.0"
  }
}
```

next.config.js

```
const withCSS = require('@zeit/next-css')
module.exports = withCSS({})
```

pages/api/TestAPI.js

```
const data = {
    name: 'Jhon Doe',
    address: '7th Avenue, Brooklyn',
    contact: '099251456',
    bloodgroup: 'A +ve',
    favouriteSnack: 'Hotdog',
    vehicle: 'Hyundai Tucson'
  }

export default (req, res) => {
    res.statusCode = 200
    res.setHeader('Content-Type', 'application/json')
    res.end(JSON.stringify(data))
}
```

pages/index.js

```
import React from "react";
import axios from 'axios';
import "../style.css";

export default class extends React.Component {
  static async getInitialProps() {
    try {
      const res = await axios.get('http://localhost:3000/api/testapi');
      return { data: res.data, error: null }
    } catch (e) {
      return { data: ", error: e }
    }
  }
```

```
render() {
  return (
    <div>
      <h1>Hello, world!</h1>
      <table>
        {Object.keys(this.props.data).map((key, index) => (
          <tr key={index}>
            <td>{key}:</td>
            <td>{this.props.data[key]}</td>
          </tr>
        ))}
      </table>
    </div>
  );
  }
}
```

In this application, we are creating a Next.js API and consuming it on the index page of our application. While consuming the API, we are using "localhost" in the API URL. This will not work in the production environment. So, let us add environment variables and use them in code. Add a ".env" file with the following code that will contain our environment variables:

.env

```
URL_TestAPI_Dev = http://localhost:3000/api/testapi
URL_TestAPI_Prod = http://www.testapplication001.com/api/testapi
```

Now, the ".env" file is currently unknown to our application. We will have to add some code in the webpack configuration of our application. We will also have to add the "dotenv-webpack" plugin to our application by executing the following command from the terminal:

```
npm install dotenv-webpack path --save
```

We have already used the "next.config.js" file to add our custom CSS loader to the webpack. We will use the same file to add the configuration for the ".env" file to the webpack. Add the following code to the "next.config.js" file:

next.config.js

```
const withCSS = require('@zeit/next-css')

require('dotenv').config();
const path = require('path');
const Dotenv = require('dotenv-webpack');

module.exports = withCSS({
    webpack(config, options){
        config.plugins = config.plugins || [];
        config.plugins = [
            ...config.plugins,
            new Dotenv({
                path: path.join(__dirname, '.env'),
                systemvars: true
            })
        ]
        return config;
    }
})
```

Once the configuration is done, any variable that we add to the ".env" file will be available throughout the application. Let us now modify our "index.js" file to use the API URL dynamically based on the application environment. If you have worked with a Node.js application before, you would be aware that Node provides a static class "Process" that provides us access to the user environment in a property called "env". We will use this class to determine the application environment. Consider the following changes to the "index.js" file:

pages/index.js

```
...
  static async getInitialProps() {
    try {
      const res = await axios.get('http://localhost:3000/api/testapi');
      return { data: res.data, error: null }
```

```
    } catch (e) {
      return { data: ", error: e }
    }
  }

  static getAPIURL(){
    if(process.env.NODE_ENV === 'production'){
      return process.env.URL_TestAPI_Prod;
    }
    else{
      return process.env.URL_TestAPI_Dev;
    }
  }

  render() {
    return (
      <div>
        <h1>
          Hello from {process.env.NODE_ENV} server
        </h1>
        <table>
          ...
        </table>
      </div>
    );
  }
...
```

When we launch the application using "npm start" command, we shall see an output similar to Figure 6-1. The data is fetched from the Next.js API that is a part of our application. This is because the "npm start" command runs the application on a local server in the development environment. We will also see the environment (development) printed in the header. We will test the same for the production environment once we deploy the application.

> # Hello from
> # development server
>
> name: Jhon Doe
> address: 7th Avenue, Brooklyn

Figure 6-1. *Application in Development Environment*

That is it about setting the environment variables. Let us now learn about Docker.

Introduction to Docker

Docker is a platform that allows us to package and execute our applications in containers that run directly on the host machine. This allows us to run multiple containerized applications simultaneously on a single host. This is particularly useful when we need to run applications targeted for different operating systems. Particularly in such scenarios, we will have to create virtual machines for each of the operating systems and then deploy our applications to their respective virtual machines. However, using Docker containers, this would not be the case. Since Docker containers directly interact with the host machine's kernel, they do not need the extra load of a hypervisor (virtual machine). We simply need to create an image of our applications which will be used to create a container for our application. This containerized application will then run, alongside other containerized applications, on the Docker engine on Host OS. That is how you would be able to run applications targeted for different operating systems on a single host machine using Docker. The difference between containerized application and virtual machine implementation can be seen in Figure 6-2.

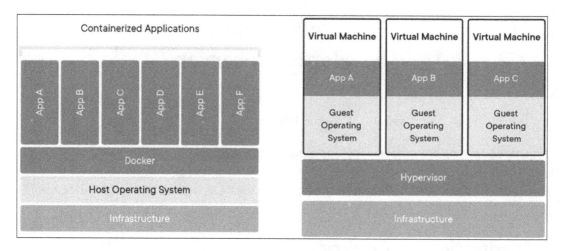

Figure 6-2. *Containerized Application vs. Virtual Machine Implementation*

There are multiple components included in the Docker architecture that can be seen in Figure 6-3. Let us briefly understand each one of them:

- **Docker Client** – This is how users communicate with Docker. It provides commands that invoke the Docker API, which can be used to communicate with Docker daemon.

- **Docker daemon** – This is part of the Docker host that listens for API requests and manages objects such as containers and images. It can also communicate with other daemons.

- **Images** – A Docker Image is a read-only template with a layered set of instructions that are used to create a Docker Container. We can create our own image or use the one created by others and published to the Registry.

- **Containers** – A Docker Container is an instance of a Docker Image. We can perform operations such as start, stop, move, or delete on the container using the Docker API or CLI.

- **Registry** – A Docker registry stores Docker images. Docker Hub is a public registry that anyone can use. Docker is configured to look for images on Docker Hub by default. You can run your own private registry as well. When you run the "docker run" or "docker pull" command, the required images are pulled from your configured registry. When you run the "docker push" command, your image is pushed to your configured registry.

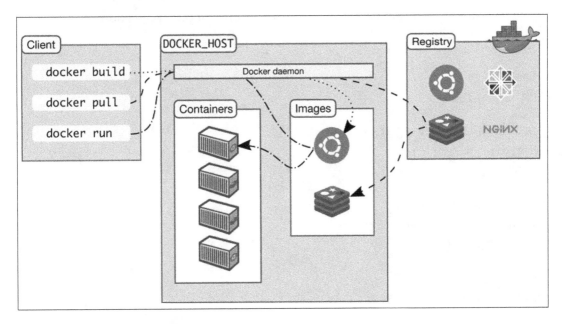

Figure 6-3. *Docker Architecture*

There are many more things that one can learn about the Docker platform. However, we will not go into the details since this chapter is about deployment and not about Docker. Let us learn how to containerize our application.

Creating a Docker Container for Your App

First of all, we will need to install Docker Desktop on our machine. It is available for Windows as well as Mac. We will need to sign up for Docker at https://hub.docker.com/. Once we sign up, we can log in to our account and visit the dashboard to find the download link for Docker Desktop. Once downloaded, you can install it on your machine like any other software. Since I am working on the Windows operating system, I have downloaded Docker Desktop for Windows. To check if it has been correctly installed on our system, we can use the following command in the terminal to check the version of Docker:

```
docker --version
```

Now, let us get back to our project. We will have to add a "Dockerfile" to the root directory of our application with the following set of instructions that will act as the Image template and will be used to create the container for our application:

Dockerfile

```
# base image
FROM node:alpine

# create & set working directory
RUN mkdir -p /usr/src
WORKDIR /usr/src

# Install dependencies
COPY package.json /usr/src
RUN npm install

# Bundle app source
COPY . /usr/src

# start app

RUN npm run build
EXPOSE 3000

CMD ["npm", "start"]
```

Let us understand what is happening here. Firstly, we are instructing Docker to start with "alpine", which is a generic implementation of Linux. Then we create a new source directory and switch to it. We copy the "package.json" file to the new source directory and install all the dependencies to it. Finally, we copy the files from our node application to the new source directory. Then we build the application, expose the port on which the node server runs, and start the server.

However, we will need to modify our "package.json" file. Make sure that you have the following scripts in your file:

package.json

```
...
"scripts": {
  "dev": "next",
  "build": "next build",
  "start": "next start"
},
...
```

Once the "Dockerfile" is in place with all the instruction, we can create a Docker image for our application using the following command provided by Docker:

```
docker build -t myfirstdockerrepo .
```

Before executing this command, make sure that Docker Desktop is running on your system. One of the common problems with Docker Desktop is the error – "unable to launch due to insufficient memory". If you run into a similar problem, try decreasing the amount of memory allocated to Docker by navigating to Docker ➤ Settings ➤ Resources. Once Docker is up and running, execute the abovementioned command. Depending on your machine and size of the application, it might take a few minutes to build a Docker image for your application. Once the command gets successfully executed, you can see all the available Docker Images using the following command:

```
docker images
```

Note that we have specified the repository name using the target option (–t) along with the "docker build" command. The name we specified is used as a tag to the Docker Image and can be used to refer to the Image Container. Note that Docker Containers are nothing but live instances of Docker Images. So when we execute the "docker images" command, the list we see is a list of Docker Containers. The terms "Image" and "Containers" are often used interchangeably. However, do not get confused. On executing the command, we shall see a list of Containers similar to Figure 6-4.

REPOSITORY	TAG	IMAGE ID	CREATED	SIZE
myfirstdockerrepo	latest	e65d07125579	13 minutes ago	319MB
node	alpine	b809734bb743	7 days ago	113MB

Figure 6-4. *Docker Containers*

That is it. We have successfully created a container for our application. Let us now learn how to host a Docker Container.

Hosting the Container

Let us first publish the image that we created locally to the Docker Hub. Before we can push the container to Docker Hub, we need to log in to the Docker Hub. To do so, execute the following command from the terminal:

```
docker login
```

If you are already logged in to the Docker Desktop on your system, the preceding command should authenticate you automatically. If not, you will be asked for your login credentials. Once logged in, we can use the "push" command to publish our container. But before that, we need to prefix the repository name of our container with our Docker username. This is because Docker automatically generates the URL for creating a repository to publish your container. If you do not prefix your repository name, Docker will automatically try to create a repository on docker.io/library and we do not have access to create a repository on a public domain. Hence, without prefixing the repository name, we will run into an authentication error. Let us add the prefix using the following commands:

```
docker tag e65 msthakkar121/myfirstdockerrepo
docker tag e65 msthakkar121/myfirstdockerrepo
```

What we are doing here is that we add a tag name to the existing container and then remove the old tag name. "e65" is the first three characters of our Image ID, which is all that we need in this case.

Note   "msthakkar121" is my Docker ID so I have used that as a prefix. However, you need to use your respective Docker IDs.

Once the repository name is prefixed and we are logged in to Docker, we need to use the following command to push the container to Docker Hub:

```
docker push msthakkar121/myfirstdockerrepo:latest
```

On successful execution of the preceding command, a public repository will be created on Docker Hub, linked to our profile. We can verify this by visiting https://hub. docker.com/ and logging in with our credentials. On visiting the "Repositories" page, we shall see "myfirstdockerrepo" added to the list. The same is shown in Figure 6-5.

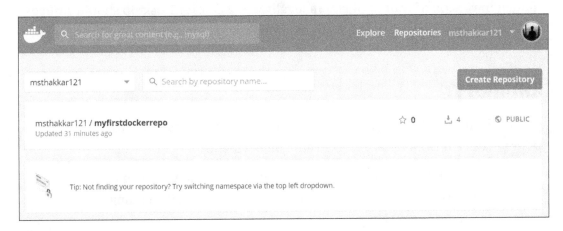

Figure 6-5. *Repositories on Docker Hub*

Now in order to run our container, we need to use the following command:

```
docker run -p 3000:3001 -d msthakkar121/myfirstdockerrepo
```

This command will run the production version of our application on our system. We specify two ports in the command using the "–p" option. The first port is for command-line operations, and the second one is for the web application. On successful execution of the command, the application will be up and running on port 3001. You can verify that by visiting the URL "http://localhost:3001/" on your browser. The output should be similar to Figure 6-6.

> # Hello from
> # production server

Figure 6-6. *Application in Production Environment*

As you can see, the environment variable that we printed on the header on our index page is now showing "production" instead of "development". This asserts that our application is successfully running on a production server. Note that the API data is presently not being fetched because we have not yet hosted our application on a public-facing cloud. You can use the services provided by platforms like DigitalOcean (`www.digitalocean.com/`) in order to host your containerized application to a public-facing cloud. However, if you have created this application for learning purposes and do not want to spend bucks on hosting services, running the production version of your application locally using Docker Desktop should suffice.

With that, we come to the end of this chapter. Let us summarize what we have learned.

Summary

- Deploying our application to a production server is essential to make sure it is working as expected after deployment.

- We need to define some environment variables and use them in the code to change the application behavior on runtime depending on the environment it is running on.

- To containerize our application, we have used Docker.

- Containerized applications interact directly with the host machine's kernel and hence do not need a hypervisor.

- Due to containerization, multiple applications targeted for different operating systems can run simultaneously on the same host machine without any hypervisor.

- We specify instructions to build a Docker container in a file called "Dockerfile" which resides in the root directory of our application.

- Then we use the "docker build" command to build a Docker container based on the instructions in "Dockerfile".

- The container can be tested in a locally simulated production environment using the "docker run" command.

- Services like "DigitalCloud" can be used to publish our application to a public-facing cloud.

Index

A

Axios (jQuery AJAX), 77–80

B

Babel configuration, 87–91

C

Cascading Style Sheets (CSS), 81–82
Client-side rendering, 139–141
Containerized application *vs.* Virtual
    machine implementation, 182

D

Deployment process
  Docker
    architecture, 182–183
    containerized and virtual
     implementation, 181
    containers, 183, 186
    Dockerfile, 184
    package.json file, 185
    repositories, 187
  environment variables, 176–178
    application, 181
    index.js file, 177–179
    next.config.js file, 178
    package.json, 176
    TestAPI.js, 177

host container, 186–188
  steps, 175
Document object model (DOM), 31–33

E, F

ECMAScript (ES), 1

G

GraphQL
  API response, 135
  getInitialProps() method, 133
  index.js, 132
  parameters, 131
  query variables, 131
  TestAPI.js, 132–135

H, I

Hot module replacement (HMR), 94

J, K, L

JavaScript application
  arithmetic operators, 16
  arrays
    definition, 22
    methods, 23–24
    output of, 25–26
    properties and methods, 24
    storing objects, 23

189

M. Thakkar, *Building React Apps with Server-Side Rendering*, https://doi.org/10.1007/978-1-4842-5869-9